"Kathleen Cahalan and Laura Kelly Fanucci offer a comprehensive, practical, and dynamic approach to the components of Christian discipleship. The authors skillfully navigate an area that is often subjected to program development and market trends, instead offering skills for the way of discipleship rooting in Christ's call and the lifelong following of his way. This is a text that will be equally effective when read and reflected upon by individuals, parish small groups, or in theology classrooms."

—Larry Fraher, director of faith formation and education at Blessed Sacrament Roman Catholic Parish, Scottsdale, Arizona

"*Called on the Way* is a highly accessible invitation to discipleship, with Kathleen Cahalan and Laura Kelly Fanucci as gentle and wise guides. The book describes what it means to be a 'called disciple on the way' in clear language, amplified by Scripture, stories of saints, the authors' own narratives, and helpful reflection questions at the end of each chapter. The book brings the authors' many years of work on vocation to a broad audience; this is a faith-filled, intelligent book for individuals or small groups, highly recommended."

—Claire Wolfteich, Boston University

"Much pastoral literature on discipleship tends to focus on one dimension of Christian life at the expense of others. Not *Called on the Way,* which is an integrative initiation into the art of discipleship inspired by a Catholic vision of the world. Each of the chapters witnesses the gift of a relationship with Jesus Christ. The book is practical but grounded in the fruit of contemplation of the Word of God. I recommend this book for parishes and individuals alike who want to follow the way of Jesus Christ more fruitfully."

—Timothy P. O'Malley, academic director, Notre Dame Center for Liturgy

Called on the Way

The Daily Practice of Discipleship

Kathleen A. Cahalan
and
Laura Kelly Fanucci

LITURGICAL PRESS
Collegeville, Minnesota
litpress.org

Cover design by Emma Elzinger, Inksplatter Design. Cover art by Susan Wilkinson (unsplash.com).

Unless otherwise noted, Scripture quotations are from New Revised Standard Version Bible © 1989 National Council of the Churches of Christ in the United States of America. Used by permission. All rights reserved worldwide.

This book is an updated and revised edition of *Living Your Discipleship: Seven Ways to Express Your Deepest Calling* published by Twenty-Third Publications in 2015.

Library of Congress Cataloging-in-Publication Data

Names: Cahalan, Kathleen A., author. | Fanucci, Laura Kelly, author.
Title: Called on the way : the daily practice of discipleship / Kathleen A. Cahalan and Laura Kelly Fanucci.
Description: Collegeville, Minnesota : Liturgical Press, [2024] | Summary: "In Called on the Way: The Daily Practice of Discipleship, authors Kathleen Cahalan and Laura Kelly Fanucci explore through personal stories, Scripture readings, and prayer experiences, what it means to be called a disciple "on the way." Called on the Way includes seven practical ways individuals can understand and live out the call to discipleship as a follower, worshiper, witness, neighbor, forgiver, prophet, and steward. Each chapter includes a personal story, biblical foundation, and connections to saintly and sacramental practice. Also includes reflection questions"— Provided by publisher.
Identifiers: LCCN 2023048792 (print) | LCCN 2023048793 (ebook) | ISBN 9798400801174 (trade paperback) | ISBN 9798400801181 (epub) | ISBN 9798400801396 (pdf)
Subjects: LCSH: Christian life. | BISAC: RELIGION / Christian Ministry / Discipleship | RELIGION / Christianity / Catholic
Classification: LCC BV4501.3 .C23 2024 (print) | LCC BV4501.3 (ebook) | DDC 248.4—dc23/eng/20240116
LC record available at https://lccn.loc.gov/2023048792
LC ebook record available at https://lccn.loc.gov/2023048793

To our families,
our first school of discipleship

Contents

Chapter 1

Called to Be Disciples in Christ

Kathleen A. Cahalan

As he was walking along, he saw Levi son of Alphaeus sitting at the tax booth, and he said to him, "Follow me." And he got up and followed him.

Mark 2:14

When I was in sixth grade, I wanted to read the whole Bible. Rather than start from Genesis, I thought I'd try another book, one I was not familiar with. I started at Ecclesiastes. Truth be told, I didn't stick with it. I couldn't figure it out—probably because it is not a book intended for children. But the desire to know God through reading the Bible has never left me. I still find reading the Bible to be central to my personal prayer life. God has sent this Word for us to enjoy and to live by, according to the words of the prophet Isaiah.

It was through reading the Bible that I came to realize the importance of discipleship. I was writing a book about ministry for students that I teach, and I had to answer the question: so why ministry? Why do we have it in the church?

I turned to the Bible and found this answer: discipleship. To be Christ's disciple, a member of the community of disciples, is central to the gospels and the early life of the church. The disciples call forth leaders to help them live the life of discipleship. This is the story of Christian faith and ministry in a nutshell.

Our calling by Christ to be his disciples is so fundamental to our faith that we sometimes fail to realize its meaning. What does it mean to be called? What is a disciple? In this book, we want to explore the meaning of being a called disciple on the way. To begin, I discuss each of these ideas: what we mean by "called," the importance of being a disciple for the early Christian community, and the image of "the way" as the central biblical theme of our journey together.

To Be Called

Think of "call" as a verb: something we do, or better yet, something God does. God has to call out to Abraham and Sarah, summon Moses, command the Israelites, and rouse the prophets. God is a caller first and foremost. To call out to us is the way God invites us to be in relationship. Through Jesus' life and ministry, God continues this dynamic movement of calling people and waiting to see how they respond. Here in flesh and blood is the God of salvation calling out to us once again: come and live in my ways, heed my commands, follow this path, and you too will be my children.

Calling is about relationship: what goes on between the One who calls and the one who responds. But relationships are two-way streets. We also call to God—crying out, shouting, asking, inviting, and begging. I have even commanded at times: "God, you must do this!" The nature of the divine–human relationship is that we call out to each other. Read one story in the Bible or read them all—the dynamic is the same. As a child I didn't need to read the whole Bible in order to understand its meaning. It is one big calling story about God's relentless love and mercy toward the people, and the people's responses, sometimes following and at other times rejecting the ways of the Lord. God first calls us into relationship, and the rest is history.

Now think of "call" as a noun—to have a call or calling or vocation (*vocare* in the Latin, meaning "calling"). In this sense, call is something we have, something we are. We each have a calling to follow Christ, received in our baptisms. We also have particular callings. For example, one of my callings is to be a teacher, and one of my coauthor Laura's callings is to be a writer. We are both called to be daughters and spouses. Laura is called to be a mother. Through our roles and relationships, each of us is blessed with many callings to heed God's invitation to follow in the way of Christ.

Calling, then, is something we do, someone we are, and someone we become.

Called to Be Disciples

"Disciple" is clearly the most prevalent term used in the New Testament to identify followers of Jesus. It appears about two hundred sixty times in the gospels and Acts of the Apostles. Disciple literally means a "pupil" or "learner" and was used in ancient times to designate a "follower of a great leader," "one who follows after," and "one who learns." It referred to followers of other religious leaders such as John the Baptist, as well as the Pharisees, all of whom had "disciples" who followed their teachings. This is true in our time as well when we follow someone we deem to be a great teacher, such as a radio personality, a politician, or a preacher.

When compared to these other teachers, Jesus is unique in that he chooses his group of disciples, rather than the more common practice by which disciples chose their teacher. At the outset of each gospel, Jesus calls by name a group to follow him. When he calls someone to follow, he asks them to give up everything. Discipleship entails a radical conversion. There is no going back.

After Jesus' death and resurrection, his disciples became known as "those of the way," which referred to people, primarily Jews, who accepted salvation through Jesus Christ. The terms "disciple" and "those of the way" identified a person as a member of a group who claimed Jesus as their teacher and the way of life they had taken up in accepting his teaching over that of others. This amazing teacher was proclaimed to be Lord and Messiah by followers of "the way."

Called on the Way

The idea that we are called "on the way" to be disciples of Jesus has deep roots in the Bible. In the Old Testament it has three primary references. The first is the Israelites' journey through the wilderness. This is "the way" of their redemption: to come out of slavery, to pass through the Red Sea, to journey for years in the wilderness, and to come to the promised land. It turns out to be a long way. They are called to trust that Yahweh—not other gods or idols—is the God of their salvation. God sends them a sign as a promise of divine faithfulness: "The LORD went in front of them in a pillar of cloud by day, to lead them along the way, and in a pillar of fire by night, to give them light, so that they might travel by day and by night" (Exodus 13:21). Through fire and cloud, God is out in front of the Israelites, never abandoning them on the path they must follow. God is their protector and shield, their rock and fortress.

A second meaning of "the way" is captured in the Psalms and refers to two paths, the way of sin and the way of goodness: "[F]or the LORD watches over the way of the righteous,

/ but the way of the wicked will perish" (Psalm 1:6). There are many ways to follow that lead us away from God's path, but this psalm makes it plain: our sinfulness leads to our own destruction. Only God's way is *the* way. Elsewhere, the psalmist prays, "See if there is any wicked way in me, and lead me in the way everlasting" (Psalm 139:24).

A final meaning of "the way" refers to God as teacher and to us as pupils. The psalmist reminds us that God longs to teach: "Good and upright is the LORD; / therefore he instructs sinners in the way. . . . He will teach them the way that they should choose" (Psalm 25:8, 12).

In the Gospel of Mark, we find all three of these meanings of "the way." In the middle section of this gospel, Jesus leaves Galilee and takes a journey with his disciples to Jerusalem. Mark is such a master storyteller that you can find six references to "on the way" in this section. Like the Israelites, the way refers to those people who walked with Jesus on his journey to the cross. But Mark also uses "the way" as a symbol for the whole journey of Christian discipleship: our turning away from sin and accepting Jesus as our teacher.

Mark spells out how the disciples get their calling wrong in a story that takes place on the way to Jerusalem. Jesus asks the disciples "on the way . . . 'Who do people say that I am?'" (Mark 8:27). But the disciples are fighting and arguing among themselves, and they can't answer this question that they should be able to answer, since they have been with him in Galilee. And what are they arguing about? Which of them is the greatest! The journey goes on, with Jesus telling them that he "must undergo great suffering and be rejected" and die, but that he will rise again in three days. In fact, he has to tell them this basic fact three times while "they are on the road," and each time they reject the message.

This part of the journey ends at Jericho, where Jesus encounters Bartimaeus, a blind man who recognizes Jesus as the Son of David and begs for mercy. Jesus says, "Call him here," and the crowd tells him, "He is calling you." Bartimaeus, "throwing off his cloak," runs to Jesus, and Jesus asks him what he wants. The blind man says, "My teacher, let me see again." Jesus replies, "Go; your faith has made you well. Immediately he regained his sight and followed him on the way" (Mark 10:46-52).

Obviously, Mark likes this twist: the disciples are indeed blind. They are on the way with Jesus, but they don't see who he is. But the blind man who cannot see is the one who knows Jesus and responds to him in faith. He is the one who truly follows Jesus on the way as a disciple. Mark is telling us that we don't know who Jesus is until we really begin to follow on the road. Once on the road, we listen to Jesus' teachings. But even when we think we start to get it, our ignorance prevails. Following Jesus requires a whole new level of learning and insight. It means grasping that this journey entails suffering and makes its way to the cross.

The amazing thing about the gospel portraits of the disciples is that these are the very people who form the church. By the power of the Holy Spirit, these men and women—most of whom could not figure out what "following" meant—are the ones who are transformed by their Easter faith and are ready to follow to their own deaths. They are the ones who proclaim that Jesus is "the way, and the truth, and the life" (John 14:6).

God's word does not return to him until it is fulfilled (Isaiah 55:11).

Called to Be a Catholic Christian on the Way

Laura and I both come from Catholic families and as adults have made our faith home in the Catholic Church. We have found in the Catholic tradition a community of disciples who can support us to follow "the way" of Jesus. We are writing this book for a Catholic audience, but we hope that it will reach Protestant and Orthodox readers as well. We invite those readers to make sense of discipleship from within their traditions, just as in this book we lean into the Catholic tradition as the home in which we discern our call to discipleship.

But honestly, *discipleship* is not very Catholic language. It is not a term either of us heard growing up in Catholic parishes or schools. The tradition adopted other terms such as "the laity" or "religious" (for those who take vows in a community) or "the clergy" (for ordained deacons, priests, and bishops). These are important distinctions in our community, but we must remember that they rest on a common baptism. And it is to that common calling that the biblical language of discipleship points. We are talking in this book about our shared vocation and our common way of life as disciples.

I stumbled into the importance of discipleship through writing a book about ministry. I wanted to say what made the calling to ministry for priests, deacons, and lay ecclesial ministers distinctive from other callings, such as an air-traffic controller, coach, or journalist. What I came to realize was that the call to ministry is the call to nurture everyone's calling in the community. It means helping all the members of the Body of Christ live out our callings to be disciples and to do this in all the many ways that God calls us—in family life and other relationships, in work and jobs, in neighborhoods and society.

When you become a disciple, you start to live in a certain way, become a certain kind of person, and take on certain practices. For example, people who follow Jesus become worshipers. When they understand that Jesus is the Incarnate One, the Messiah who will save them, they call him "Lord" and fall down at his feet. When he heals them and converts them away from sin, they want to proclaim this good news. They become witnesses. To be a worshiper and witness means learning to be a neighbor to family and friends as well as to strangers and enemies. When a follower is called to be a neighbor, he or she is called to be a forgiver. For followers of Jesus, the call to be neighbor and forgiver means being a prophet, concerned for all the harm and violence that befalls neighbors. And finally, to be a follower is to be a steward, one who cares for God's creation as well as for the "household" of faith.

Discipleship, then, consists of seven features: follower, worshiper, witness, neighbor, forgiver, prophet, and steward. We will elaborate on each feature by drawing out stories from Scripture, stories from our lives and the lives of those we know, and stories from the saints' lives. We also connect each feature to one of the seven sacraments. We do not mean, however, that discipleship is seven different things; rather, the call to follow Jesus takes on particular shape as he calls us into relationship.

Called to Work Together

In 2009, we were called to work together on figuring out what calling and vocation mean for Christians. Together we led the Collegeville Institute Seminars at the Collegeville Institute on the campus of Saint John's University and Abbey in Collegeville, Minnesota, from 2009 until 2018. In our seminars, we studied and discerned the meaning of vocation and calling, especially as it relates to people's work in the world and as it relates to the entire span of our lives, from infants to older adults. Obviously, we love the idea of calling—we've been working on it for years.

Kathleen is a professor of practical theology at Saint John's University School of Theology and Seminary. She teaches people preparing for ministry—those whose calling it is to call forth the life of discipleship in each of us. She first developed the seven features of discipleship in her 2010 book on ministry, *Introducing the Practice of Ministry*.

Laura earned a master of divinity at Saint John's School of Theology in 2006. She served as the research associate of the

Collegeville Institute Seminars and directed the Institute's *Communities of Calling* project from 2018 to 2020. She is the founder of *Mothering Spirit*, where she first started writing about parenting and spirituality in 2010 (www.motheringspirit.com), and the author of small-group programs *Called to Life* and *Called to Work* (appendix 3).

We wrote this book collaboratively, planning each chapter's stories and contents, and we each had a hand in authoring particular chapters. Kathleen wrote "Called to Be Disciples in Christ," "Follower," "Witness," and "Forgiver"; Laura wrote "Worshiper," "Neighbor," "Prophet," "Steward," and the conclusion.

There are many social and political issues today that demand that disciples of Christ discern a response; for instance, what are our callings in light of changing global climate patterns, violence against persons of color, deadly pandemics, the erosion of democracy, and the unknown impact of emerging artificial intelligence technology? We decided not to address broad social, cultural, and political challenges—a task for another book—because each of these are particular and contextual to each of our lives and the lives of your parish and community. We think what is most needed is to practice discernment about how to respond in the place that we are.

And, of course, that is not the whole story when you stand at this place and time as a disciple of Christ. There is also so much good news about what God is calling people to do to counter rising sea and land temperatures, mending the social fabric between diverse racial groups, securing the right to vote for everyone, and stewarding technological advances to fight disease and pandemics. We find hope in the resurrection, even as our churches have undergone significant changes, both positive and negative, that have impacted our lives as disciples. Declining church attendance and polarization within parishes may challenge our sense of belonging, though we long ever more deeply for the support of local communities of faith and the hope of the resurrection amid all of today's upheavals.

Rather than try to account for all these challenges and graces, we are inviting you to bring your questions and insights from both the global and the local levels as you consider the life of discipleship today, because on the one hand the call to discipleship is enduring: God calls us to follow Christ in the place that we are, and no doubt you, like us, are in a different place than you were ten years ago. Take the pandemic, for example. You may be someone for whom the pandemic brought tremendous loss, whether in work and income, or through the death of someone you know and love. Laura found herself in February of 2020 with preeclampsia just weeks away from delivering a baby boy. She gave birth and, after a long stay in the hospital, she and her husband brought Isaiah home to his four brothers. Within two weeks they were shut up in the house—school at home on Zoom, both parents working on Zoom, and a mother and newborn who were both recovering and needing to be protected from the virus. That was a hard time in Laura's life. What was God calling her to? As this book goes to press, Laura is facing treatment, surgery, and radiation for breast cancer. How is God calling her to follow on his path in this time and place?

You see, following Christ is in all the stuff of our ordinary, daily lives, even traumatic pregnancies and serious diagnoses, as well as enjoying a newborn's first smile, making a meal for our family, writing our congressional representatives, protesting injustice, and joining others to worship on Sunday; this is where God meets us and where God calls us to respond. The path is no easier today than it was in the past, but it may be different because of where we find ourselves.

As Christians we share a common calling in Christ, regardless of the particular ups and downs of our story. We are first a community of disciples, sharing a common calling. Our framework in this book—the seven features of discipleship—are one way of saying we are united in Christ by seeking to follow him together, and we want to challenge ourselves to consider what our communal responses to the signs of the times are.

At the same time, each of our lives is quite particular. I did not experience the pandemic as a great hardship. In fact, I had already been teaching online and found that it was quite easy to make a few adjustments and keep going. My husband and I spent at least six months in 2020 and 2021 at our home on Lake Superior, a place where my spiritual life is nurtured and renewed in the beauty of the wilderness. I found a whole new dimension of my calling to live the contemplative life when the outside world shut down. God called me to a new ministry in March 2020—leading the practice of *lectio divina* on a just-launched app called Ritual - Wellbeing Practices, something I had not anticipated just weeks earlier. What's particular about your own story of calling during times of social change, personal struggle, and surprising events?

Reading *Called on the Way* Together

This book can be read on your own or in a small group. We have included several reflection questions at the end of each chapter, which will help you draw out and identify how you and your parish and community can live the life of discipleship in the time and place where God is leading you in truth and calling you now. You might feel compelled to write out your answers in a journal or to share your insights with others. If you are interested in forming a small group, we have provided a resource at the end of the book that includes a format and process for a meeting (appendix 2).

Our writing and teaching are forged in prayer, in particular the practice of *lectio divina* or "holy reading" of Scripture.

We can't figure out any other way to stay on the path of discipleship but to listen closely to God's word. We therefore invite you into the practice of prayerful discernment about God's call to be a disciple of Christ. Each chapter of *Called on the Way* opens with a Scripture passage related to one of the seven features of discipleship. Instead of simply reading this Scripture story and continuing on to the rest of the chapter, we hope you will sit with the word of God in a prayerful way through *lectio divina*, asking that your heart may be opened to see how you are called.

The practice of *lectio divina* is a slow, quiet encounter with Scripture that has been used by Christians for centuries. St. Benedict described this prayerful study of Scripture in his Rule of St. Benedict, written in the sixth century. Reading and reflecting on a biblical passage three times allows God's word to move from our lips, to our minds, and finally into our hearts. (Appendix 1 offers a step-by-step guide to *lectio divina*.) Over time, this prayer practice can open our eyes and ears to discern how God is speaking to us in our everyday lives, calling us to be disciples. We hope that through your practice of *lectio divina*, God's word will not return empty, but will accomplish God's purposes in your life as you respond to the call to follow Jesus on the way.

Chapter 2

Follower

Kathleen A. Cahalan

As he walked by the Sea of Galilee, he saw two brothers, Simon, who is called Peter, and Andrew his brother, casting a net into the sea—for they were fishermen. And he said to them, "Follow me, and I will make you fish for people." Immediately they left their nets and followed him. As he went from there, he saw two other brothers, James son of Zebedee and his brother John, in the boat with their father Zebedee, mending their nets, and he called them. Immediately they left the boat and their father, and followed him.

Jesus went throughout Galilee, teaching in their synagogues and proclaiming the good news of the kingdom and curing every disease and every sickness among the people. So his fame spread throughout all Syria, and they brought to him all the sick, those who were afflicted with various diseases and pains, demoniacs, epileptics, and paralytics, and he cured them. And great crowds followed him from Galilee, the Decapolis, Jerusalem, Judea, and from beyond the Jordan.

When Jesus saw the crowds, he went up the mountain; and after he sat down, his disciples came to him. Then he began to speak, and taught them, saying . . .

Matthew 4:18–5:2

Called by Name

This guy is on the move.

The opening scene of Jesus' ministry after his baptism is all action: he walks, calls, teaches, proclaims, cures, hikes, sits down, and speaks. If you are going to follow, you have to get up and get going, even if you are in the middle of something, such as casting (or surfing) the net.

I often marvel when I read this story; it is so abrupt that it is almost unbelievable. Who would really leave their job and the things they need for work, like a boat and nets, which likely took these men a great deal of time and effort to obtain? And who would leave the fish? They probably need to sell them, or at least take them home for their families to eat. But then the story makes me want to scream. What about their father? Do they really just leave him to fend for himself? I could never do that.

But if you don't follow immediately, you will miss it: you won't hear his teaching or witness him cure the sick or see the great crowds coming or finally sit at his feet to listen.

In baptism we enter the great drama of the Christian life—the taking up to follow, the leaving behind—in order to learn from the great teacher and healer. And we always enter the scene midstream. The action is already taking place, and we must come along wherever we are and drop whatever it is we are doing.

When a child is baptized, the parents are asked, "What name do you give this child?" and "What do you ask of God's Church?" My parents answered, "Kathleen." And they asked of the Catholic Church, "Faith." Many Catholics were baptized as infants, so we did not choose to follow—others chose for us. Our community made a promise to live as Christ's followers and to teach us what discipleship entails. In this sense, discipleship is a gift.

But discipleship is also a choice. Perhaps as a child or teen or as an adult, you had to make the choice. During the summer after my senior year of high school, I volunteered in a six-week service program. I had a funny feeling that I was being called to some kind of work with the sick or dying, but I wanted to experience something of this before I went off to college. I was disappointed when I was not sent to the hospital I wanted and ended up in Georgia assigned to teach in a Bible camp for children. I was pretty sure this was not my calling since I had no gift for teaching children. Over the course of the first few weeks, the situation was not going well for the group leader nor for me; no doubt I was constantly complaining. At the beginning of the fourth week, the leader finally told me not to attend camp that week, but to go visit the sick if that was what I wanted to do. And with that, the team left on Monday morning. I had a list of parishioners but little desire to go meet these people, most of whom were strangers. The list included Marv, a paraplegic whom we had visited in the county nursing home, but the place smelled so bad I could not return. So instead of visiting the sick, I hung around the house and slept most of the day.

One afternoon I had a dream. It was simple. I heard my name called out: "Kathleen." And I woke up. I mean I *really* woke up, and not just from the nap. I heard God shouting at me. I realized that I had only about one week left, so I grabbed the list of names and visited as many people as I could, including Marv. And when I went to college the following autumn, I wrote "Kathleen" on the registration form rather than "Kathy," the name I had been called since childhood.

As a teen growing into adulthood, I heard Christ summon me by name. I heard a call in that dream, and I had a choice to make—I could follow or not. That time I followed, though this has not always been the case.

Discovering Our Calling Stories

Everyone has "call stories"—a time when God sought us out and we had to respond. The problem is that we don't trust our own stories. I had a dramatic and quite literal wake-up call, but it doesn't always happen that way. Most call stories are quite ordinary; rather than a shout, we might hear a song or a whisper. Whatever it is, we sense it is an invitation. And sometimes it is a risk.

My friend Jane begged God to tell her what her vocation was to be. She wanted to be a Christian rock singer and wanted God to send a lightning bolt to confirm the direction of her choice. A contract from a major music studio would be a sure sign. But nothing. Finally, one day, walking alone and praying, she heard God say in her heart, "I will give you the people you need." That was it. No great epiphany on a mountain. Just the sure promise that God would be with her and the sign would be that she would have people on the way to accompany her. And she definitely found those people. Jane did not become a Christian rock star, but she did find the people she needed to figure out where she was going in professional work as an actor.

God wants to tell us something. But we need the ears to listen. We also need to know that God "speaks" in many ways. My story is about a dream; Jane's call came through prayer. Most people "hear" God's call through identifying their gifts, through an invitation by another person to do something, and through affirmation that what they can do is of real service to others.

The point is that we have to trust our own experience. God is calling out to us, summoning us, inviting us. God wouldn't do it if God didn't love us or think we could actually follow. The call to discipleship is rooted in love and trust. Remember? God chooses us first, God keeps the covenant, and it is God's mercy that endures forever. In some ways, it does not matter that I did not choose this "way" as an infant, since God has called me continuously throughout my life. I've had more than one chance to say "yes" to the call given to me at baptism. On that hot summer day in Georgia, God's voice was just what I needed to hear.

Learning to Follow Jesus

The story of Jesus and the disciples consists of roughly two parts. The first part of each gospel tells the story of the disciples' "schooling" in the way of Jesus. They are taught by him through parables and discourses, and they witness a large number of healings and exorcisms. They are eyewitnesses to who Jesus is: the in-breaking presence and future coming of God's reign. During the early part of Jesus' ministry, the disciples grow in understanding and faithfulness, being summoned to take up Jesus' ministry of healing, preaching, and teaching.

The second part of each gospel story consists of the journey toward Jerusalem and the dynamics at play when Jesus faces opposition to his teachings and way of life. A drama unfolds in which an increasing number of disciples, along with the crowd, grow weary, while some leave and some continue to follow. Along the way, there is growing opposition to Jesus from Jewish religious authorities, Roman officials, and even his own followers. As the conflicts heighten, the disciples do not always understand Jesus' teaching. They see—but do not believe in—God's mission proclaimed by him, and they are increasingly weak, ignorant, and hard of heart. One denies, another betrays, and many flee. Following becomes a more difficult choice and commitment as the route transforms into a path of suffering and death. By the time Jesus dies on the cross, only a few disciples have followed him all the way. They stand together at the foot of the cross, take down the body, anoint it, and bury him.

The gospel writers do not spare the disciples, perhaps because they knew them. Each paints a realistic picture, not in order to judge them, but because they have come to know in their own lives that discipleship is a difficult path to follow. Their own communities were struggling to embrace and endure the call of Christ, and they found in these first disciples a realistic story that bore this truth.

I too resist God's call at times. I don't want to follow. I'd rather have it my own way. There was a time at work when I ate lunch with a group of colleagues, and we got into a bad habit of scoffing. Do you know what scoffing is? It means to mock, to jeer, and to speak derisively. So it is not just gossiping—it's a step further. It is speech that destroys. Later I was praying Psalm 1 and said the words, "Happy are those who do not follow the advice of the wicked, or take the path that sinners tread, or sit in the seat of scoffers" (Psalm 1:1). I was nailed. I was a scoffer! I realized that at the lunch table, I was sitting in the seat of scoffers—deriding others, mocking and putting down people who were not there, and putting myself above all the others. My own prayer condemned me. This was not the way of discipleship. The only way I was going to turn around was to leave the table. I began eating my lunch alone. Eventually I told some colleagues what I had done, and we found another table where we could eat together. I decided I had to find a way to build up the community with good speech and action and not tear it down with my tongue.

Called in Baptism

Interestingly, the term "disciple" is rarely singular in the New Testament. It most often appears in the plural: *disciples.* Jesus does call each disciple by name, thus establishing a personal relationship, yet to be a follower is to be within a community of disciples. The calling is both personal and communal. We join together to follow, and we are each summoned as the unique person we are.

But following in a crowd or group might not sound very important or significant. It might strike us as weak, as in following the herd, or sheep that follow blindly. Aren't we supposed to be leaders, not followers? We can "follow" all kinds of conversations on the internet and "like" what we support on social media, but this kind of following may not involve us in deep relationship or commitment. There is so much that lures us to follow through false and empty promises. The other day I read on a juice bottle label: "reawaken, rebirth, repurpose, redefine." I was stunned—a bottle of juice could do all that! What a cheap use of words. The only truth from the point of view of discipleship is to be reawakened in Christ, to experience a rebirth through the waters of baptism, and to find purpose and definition in following in his way.

Called for Mission

Many followers of Jesus have done things I can't imagine doing. For example, we do not know much about St. Patrick, but his is still a great story: taken as a slave at the age of sixteen by Irish pirates and imprisoned for six years, he seeks God's forgiveness, serves as a shepherd, escapes to return home, wanders in the wilderness, attends seminary, becomes a missionary, returns to Ireland, and baptizes thousands. Whether or not every bit is factually true, his life bears a truth—his story echoes the stories of Joseph, Moses, the Israelites, David, John the Baptist, Paul, and, of course, Jesus. It is only because these stories become *his* story that Patrick embodies following Christ in such a bold and brave way.

In his memorable prayer, the Breastplate of St. Patrick, he writes,

Christ with me,
Christ before me,
Christ behind me,
Christ in me,
Christ beneath me,
Christ above me,
Christ on my right,
Christ on my left,
Christ when I lie down,
Christ when I sit down,
Christ when I arise,
Christ in the heart of everyone who thinks of me,
Christ in the mouth of everyone who speaks of me,
Christ in every eye that sees me,
Christ in every ear that hears me.

Patrick realized that to be a follower does not mean becoming a hero. It means immersing one's whole life in Christ. It may require you to cast out all the snakes on an island. But for most of us it means that, in every moment, we find our awakening, our purpose, and our identity by orienting ourselves more fully toward Christ, who is already behind, before, above, beside, and all around, like the cloud by day and the fire by night. That's what it means to embody God's mission in our lives: to follow God who is all around and out in front of us.

Following or Not

But we don't live in a time when people are eager to follow the way of Jesus. Survey results on religious participation all say the same thing: fewer people participate in church. According to a 2022 Pew Research Center survey, about 64 percent of Americans, including children, say they are Christian, about 6 percent of the population belong to other religions (mostly Jews, Muslims, Hindus, and Buddhists), and those who report being religiously unaffiliated, sometimes called religious "nones," are 30 percent of the population. We often refer to people who have left our church with labels such as "lapsed," "former," even "heretic." It's not that they don't believe in God (indeed, many do). It's that many don't believe in churches anymore or in joining a group of other followers to figure out the way. It makes sense when Christian churches have been hypocritical, greedy, and abusive.

So why stay when so many leave? Or why consider coming back if you have left? There are many reasons, but first we ought to stay with humility—not because we think we have it all right. Discipleship is a journey on the way, and in the church we find a company of disciples with whom to share the story and break the bread. We need this community to help us live out a journey on which we will surely fail and suffer. It is together that we discover the power of a new life in Christ.

Jesus the Follower

We follow the One who follows in Abba's way, for Jesus is the perfect disciple, the perfect follower. He taught disciples what it means to embrace God's mission with their whole lives when he accepted his death and placed his trust completely in God. In order to follow, we must come to him, sit at his feet, and learn how to do this. To be a follower means entering into a lifelong process of learning from Jesus, to come to know who and what Jesus is and what Jesus is claiming about God's call to community and mission.

We live, then, in Christ because Christ lives in us. To be Christ's follower is to embrace Christ as teacher, to seek wisdom and understanding for what the path and cost of discipleship entails, and to be schooled in the paschal mystery of death and new life.

Reflection Questions

- Recall your baptism. If you can, ask someone who attended it: What do they remember? What is significant to you now about being baptized on that day? What is the meaning of your name?
- How have you heard God call your name? For example, was it through another person, a situation at work or church, or a realization about your gifts?
- How is Christ calling you to follow at this point in your life?
- Look up St. Patrick's Breastplate and pray it every day for one week. What does it say to you? What would be the prayer written on your breastplate?
- When has it ever cost you to follow? Have you ever had to stand up for someone who was being harmed or rejected by others? Did you stand by and watch or stand up and help? Is God calling you to stand up for someone now?

Chapter 3

Worshiper

Laura Kelly Fanucci

When Jesus had come down from the mountain, great crowds followed him; and there was a leper who came to him and knelt before him, saying, "Lord, if you choose, you can make me clean." He stretched out his hand and touched him, saying, "I do choose. Be made clean!" Immediately his leprosy was cleansed. Then Jesus said to him, "See that you say nothing to anyone; but go, show yourself to the priest, and offer the gift that Moses commanded, as a testimony to them."

When he entered Capernaum, a centurion came to him, appealing to him and saying, "Lord, my servant is lying at home paralyzed, in terrible distress." And he said to him, "I will come and cure him." The centurion answered, "Lord, I am not worthy to have you come under my roof; but only speak the word, and my servant will be healed. For I also am a man under authority, with soldiers under me; and I say to one, 'Go,' and he goes, and to another, 'Come,' and he comes, and to my slave, 'Do this,' and the slave does it." When Jesus heard him, he was amazed and said to those who followed him, "Truly I tell you, in no one in Israel have I found such faith. I tell you, many will come from east and west and will eat with Abraham and Isaac and Jacob in the kingdom of heaven, while the heirs of the kingdom will be thrown into the outer darkness, where there will be weeping and gnashing of teeth." And to the centurion Jesus said, "Go; let it be done for you according to your faith." And the servant was healed in that hour.

Matthew 8:1-13

In the middle of Advent one year, my husband and I found out we were expecting our first child. We had been trying to have a baby for several years, and Advent had always been a difficult season for us to sit in the pews at church. The season's hymns about waiting for a child were hard to hear when our hearts were longing for a baby. But going to Mass together had become an important part of our faith life, especially as we struggled through infertility. We felt strengthened by God's presence in the Eucharist and supported by the community surrounding us. So when we discovered that we were expecting a baby, our instinct was to go back to church and give thanks to God—not simply for the life of our child, but for the faithfulness of God's love all along our journey. Worship gave us the chance to sing God's praises in good times and in hard times, and to remember ourselves back into Christ's presence.

When we turn to God in prayer, we sing with the psalmist: "O come, let us worship and bow down, / let us kneel before the LORD, our Maker!" (Psalm 95:6). As Catholics we believe that we encounter the living Christ in the sacraments, in Scripture, and in other people. But we also wonder what it would have been like to encounter Jesus while he walked the earth. Would we recognize him? Would we approach him? Would we ask him a question? Or would we simply fall on our knees in wonder?

In the Gospel of Matthew, the first people to meet Jesus (besides Mary and Joseph) are the magi, who react with amazement: "When they saw that the star had stopped, they were overwhelmed with joy. On entering the house, they saw the child with Mary his mother; and they knelt down and paid him homage. Then, opening their treasure chests, they offered him gifts of gold, frankincense, and myrrh" (Matthew 2:10-11). After years of singing "We Three Kings" at Christmastime, we can miss the truth of this strange story: wise and powerful men from another land travel far distances to worship a poor and helpless child. There is something immediately recognizable about Jesus, even from the earliest days of his life, that is worthy of worship.

Many other people in the gospels react this way when they meet Jesus face to face. The leper kneels before Jesus, humbly asking to be healed. The centurion asks Jesus to speak a word to cure his servant, though he does not feel worthy to have Jesus enter under his roof. Whether someone is a powerful leader or a social outcast, whether they are asking for their own needs or interceding on behalf of others, what matters to Jesus is the depth of their faith. Once he sees into their hearts, then he speaks with them, acknowledging how their faith is revealed in their words and actions. He notices their needs and welcomes their questions. Jesus models the relationship that worship entails: a dynamic of call and answer, a dialogue between human needs and divine response.

Jesus as Worshiper

Throughout Jesus' active ministry—and certainly in the many years of quiet work leading up to his public ministry—he prayed regularly. He sought solitude as well as the support of his friends as he gave his life in love to God. In Luke's gospel, for example, Jesus is portrayed in prayer at each significant moment of his life: beginning his ministry, doing the work of teaching and healing, entering into his passion in Jerusalem, facing his death, and dying on the cross. Jesus embodies perfect worship. He models for his disciples how to pray, and he teaches them about prayer. He offers his whole self to God in trust and hope.

Prayer for Jesus is an ongoing dialogue of communion with God. It opens Jesus' heart, mind, and soul to the source of divine love. Through prayer, Jesus offers praise and thanksgiving, asks for forgiveness for his enemies, and seeks

God's guidance and support. This is our model of worship as disciples: to enter into an ongoing dialogue with God as the foundation of our calling as Christians.

To make prayer a way of life is our goal.

Our Call to Worship

Outside of religious circles, the word "worship" has negative connotations. We judge crazed sports fans, celebrity obsessions, unhealthy relationships, or power imbalances as examples of worship gone wrong. But as followers of Christ, we believe that worship is positive. It is a primary condition of discipleship.

So how do we make worship the center of our lives as Christians?

I once attended a retreat that used one simple song as its refrain, based on a line from the Letter of James: "Humble yourselves before the Lord, and he will exalt you" (James 4:10). Throughout the three-day retreat, I kept expecting the team leaders to teach us other songs or hymns that would connect with the talks and themes of each day. But instead we sang the same refrain over and over—as we waited for meals to begin, as we walked through the woods, as we ended each day in quiet prayer.

Only years later did I realize the wisdom in centering the retreat around words of worship, humility, and hope. The Christian life calls us to turn toward God with a humble heart and a trusting faith, just like the leper and the centurion in Matthew's gospel. Catholics echo the centurion's words every time we prepare to receive the Eucharist: "Lord, I am not worthy that you should enter under my roof, but only say the word and my soul shall be healed." We believe that when we humble ourselves before Christ in worship, we can be lifted up in powerful ways.

Traditionally, Christians have worshiped God through different types of prayer: praising God in adoration, seeking God's forgiveness through confession, thanking God for blessings, and petitioning God for our needs and those of others. (These four movements of prayer are sometimes memorized with the mnemonic "ACTS": Adoration, Confession, Thanksgiving, and Supplication.)

Called to Adore

Praise of God is the beginning of all our prayer. The Catholic Church's daily prayer of the Liturgy of the Hours begins with praising God through the psalms in Morning Prayer, in order to reorient our lives each new day to God's great love, justice, and mercy. So too does our worship at Mass start with hymns of praise and the joyful refrain of the Gloria.

Dorothy Day, cofounder of the Catholic Worker Movement (now known as Servant of God since her cause for canonization has begun), once said that "worship, adoration, thanksgiving, supplication . . . were the noblest acts of which we are capable in this life."* She often spoke about how her practices of worship—including daily Mass, a daily rosary, and weekly confession—gave her the strength needed for her work with the poor. Whatever our work, we are called to begin and end our days by praising God.

For years my family has sung the doxology "Praise God, from whom all blessings flow" at the end of our grace before dinner. At first we picked this hymn because it was a simple song to teach our children as they grew. It reminded us about God as the source of all that is good in our lives. But over the years, as I have sung this prayer every night—in bright

* Jim Forest, "Servant of God Dorothy Day," CatholicWorker.org, February 11, 2022, https://catholicworker.org/servant-of-god-html/.

moods and dark moods, in celebration and lament, in joy and in sadness—I have come to appreciate how small daily habits of praise shape our faith as disciples. Even when we do not feel like rejoicing, we remember ourselves through praise back into the bigger story of God's love for us.

Called to Confess

Sometimes we mistakenly lump together "praise" and "worship," believing that worship of God includes only joy and celebration. But if worship describes our basic inner stance toward God, it must also embrace our flaws, faults, and failings. There is always space in our prayer to admit how we have fallen short of God's plan of love. We know that we need God's help to turn back in repentance.

When we prepared to receive the sacrament of reconciliation for the first time, we were taught to make an act of contrition that acknowledges our sins in light of "[our] God, who are all good and deserving of all [our] love." We speak our sins aloud not simply to air our grievances, but because we want to approach God with a clean and hopeful heart. This is why each celebration of the Mass includes a penitential act at its beginning: the *Confiteor* ("I confess to almighty God . . . ") and the litany of "Lord, have mercy / Christ, have mercy / Lord, have mercy." Before we can enter into the fullness of the joy that Christ has prepared for us, we ask for forgiveness for what we have done wrong. We can do this because we trust that the God we worship is merciful.

Called to Give Thanks

Giving thanks to God is not reserved for November or turkey dinners. The Greek word "eucharist" means thanksgiving, so we actually celebrate a feast of gratitude each time we go to Mass. Thanksgiving flows from praise as we remember God's gifts, and it follows from confession as we remember God's forgiveness.

Thanksgiving can be expressed in dramatic gestures. We have all watched athletes drop to one knee or point to heaven to thank God for their winning score. Gratitude to God can also come in smaller forms, seen in the popularity of social media "gratitude challenges" where people commit to a daily post of things for which they are thankful. No matter how we give thanks publicly, what matters to God is the humble gratitude of our hearts. (And before we grumble about the winning athlete on the opposite team, we must remember that we can never know the inner truth of someone's faith or how they express it outwardly, even in the end zone!) Whenever we thank God for our blessings, we become like the one leper who turned back to Jesus while nine others ran off in forgetful joy. We can continue on our way of discipleship with a clearer vision of how God is leading us.

Called to Pray for Others

Praying for others' needs can seem like an obvious part of our prayer life. A friend is struggling financially, a family member is going through a difficult divorce, or a coworker has a serious illness, and we offer to pray for them. At Mass we practice this kind of intercession when we offer the prayer of the faithful. We gather our concerns as a community, trusting that God will hear our prayer. Our petitions can even include laments, since worship makes room for our anger, frustration, and sorrow through the Spirit who "intercedes with sighs too deep for words" (Romans 8:26).

In college I worked for the student newspaper and once edited a column written by the friend of a student who had recently died from leukemia. In describing her grief, she wrote that she was struggling with faith in the wake of her friend's death. She was angry with God and could not pray as she once did. So she asked all those who read her words to pray for her and for all those who could not pray now, lost in their sorrow. She knew the prayers of the campus community could help carry her through her spiritual crisis even when she lacked the words or the will to pray herself.

All of us experience times of doubt or dryness in our spiritual journeys. Rituals of worship can seem empty when we do not feel the inner faith that breathes life into these actions. But if we keep practicing these external expressions of belief, we can find that our faith eventually rises up again as the community intercedes for us. Many Christians have experienced this solace in rituals surrounding death and burial. We may be so overwhelmed by grief during a loved one's funeral that we can barely pray, but the community that prays with us and for us can bring consolation during our hour of darkness.

Pray without Ceasing

The church offers us practices for praising the presence of God that are communal and personal, formal and informal, and liturgical and devotional. As Catholics, we gather to celebrate the Eucharist each week as a formal, public activity of worship. Sunday Mass unites and strengthens us as we join the whole church in praying the Creed and Our Father. Catholics also come together as a community to pray popular devotions such as the rosary, the Stations of the Cross, or eucharistic adoration.

Our personal habits of prayer are also important for discerning God's will in our life. Informal acts of worship may include offering our day to God when we first wake, singing a song or praying in silence on the drive to work, saying grace with our family before meals, or offering to remember a friend in our daily prayer. Acts of worship do not need to be elaborate to be deeply meaningful. A simple Sign of the Cross can remind us of essential truths of our faith: we believe in the Trinity as Father, Son, and Holy Spirit, and we believe the cross is central to the mystery of Christ's death and resurrection.

Whether personal or communal, private or public, formal or informal, worship is not simply an activity that we do or an obligation of our faith. It is an opportunity to encounter Christ in Scripture, sacrament, and other people. It is an ongoing invitation to recenter our lives around God. It is an identity that we grow into over a lifetime. We become what we do when we give our hearts to God in worship and ask to be transformed, week after week in worship. Like stones that are smoothed by years and years of the steady rush of flowing water, we are changed over time into people who find their home in God.

So we worship not only when we feel inspired or when our schedule allows, but in all places, times, and seasons. Paul invites us to "pray without ceasing" (1 Thessalonians 5:17), not simply when we are in need. Worship reminds us that the fundamental orientation of all our callings is toward God. If we do not nurture our relationship with God with regular attention, our lives will soon run dry. So we turn to God in worship, seeking help in following our vocations and giving thanks for how we have been lifted up by God's love.

Since early times, Christians have prayed "through Christ our Lord." This phrase can become the refrain of our callings, too—that all our lives may be given to God through Christ.

Reflection Questions

- The next time you start to pray, notice whether you praise God first or immediately jump into your requests. What happens when you begin with adoration instead of asking?
- Our practices of confession can be formal (when we seek out the sacrament of reconciliation) or informal (when we apologize to someone we have hurt). How do you invite God into your practices of confessing your sins? How can we confess our communal sins more boldly and honestly?
- The church describes the Eucharist as the "source and summit" of our life as Catholics. The next time you are at Mass, focus on giving thanks to God for this encounter with Christ. What gifts has this sacrament brought to your life? When you think back on how the pandemic impacted your parish's communal worship, what new perspectives do you bring to Mass today?
- What intercessions are at the top of your prayer list these days—for others you know? For global concerns? For your own questions related to your callings?
- Dorothy Day found a way to connect worship and a life of service and justice for the poor. What difference does it make to pray for justice in the face of injustice? What do you think is the relationship between prayer and working for justice?
- If you are interested in new practices of worship, research the Liturgy of the Hours. (Many monasteries offer resources online.) Try praying Morning Prayer or Evening Prayer or "Daily Lectio" on the Ritual - Wellbeing Practices app over the next week. Notice what starts to emerge in you as you commit yourself to this practice.

Chapter 4

Witness

Kathleen A. Cahalan

While they were talking about this, Jesus himself stood among them and said to them, "Peace be with you." They were startled and terrified, and thought that they were seeing a ghost. He said to them, "Why are you frightened, and why do doubts arise in your hearts? Look at my hands and my feet; see that it is I myself. Touch me and see; for a ghost does not have flesh and bones as you see that I have." And when he had said this, he showed them his hands and his feet. While in their joy they were disbelieving and still wondering, he said to them, "Have you anything here to eat?" They gave him a piece of broiled fish, and he took it and ate in their presence.

Then he said to them, "These are my words that I spoke to you while I was still with you—that everything written about me in the law of Moses, the prophets, and the psalms must be fulfilled." Then he opened their minds to understand the scriptures, and he said to them, "Thus it is written, that the Messiah is to suffer and to rise from the dead on the third day, and that repentance and forgiveness of sins is to be proclaimed in his name to all nations, beginning from Jerusalem. You are witnesses of these things. And see, I am sending upon you what my Father promised; so stay here in the city until you have been clothed with power from on high."

Luke 24:36-49

It hasn't been easy for Ken and Mary Margaret to figure out God's calling in their lives at this point. Ken has been diagnosed with Alzheimer's disease, and though he is in the early stages, everything has changed. His wife, Mary Margaret, was depressed and angry at the beginning: "The diagnosis of Alzheimer's was extremely painful. It took a while for me to process. I realized I had a choice to make. Either I could continue to be in pain or in suffering, or I could find the joy in the pain, become an advocate, educator, ambassador." She has also found her calling in being a caregiver. Ken has found his calling in living in the present moment. He volunteers for the Alzheimer's Association and has one message: "Don't worry about what you can't do. Do as much as you can today!" As a couple, they have had to find a calling together after being "stripped of what was important to us." Mary Margaret says, "We are walking this journey together; we are of one mind. Alzheimer's is not a blessing. It's not a curse. But many blessings have come." Their lives bear witness to the truth about who they are.

When Jesus asks his disciples, "Why are you frightened, and why do doubts arise in your hearts?" I think I would have been the one to reply, "Because, Lord, everything does not work out so great. How are we supposed to be certain that our lives are following you on the way when nothing seems very certain?"

When we live our callings, when we tell each other how God has called us, or when we admit how hard it can be to figure out what to do and what God wants—*that* is being a witness. It is telling a truth about our lives, about our certainties and our doubts, our fears and our joys.

What the disciples witness that day after the resurrection is just too good to be true. But "in their joy" they are still "disbelieving and still wondering" (Luke 24:41). That gives me hope about discipleship. When Jesus calls them to be "witnesses of these things," I sense he has in mind the whole picture: the wondrous good news that he lives and will reign at the end of time, but also our disbelieving and still wondering about what is real and what is not.

To Face the Truth

When Jesus dies on the cross, there is a Roman soldier on the scene: "Now when the centurion, who stood facing him, saw that in this way he breathed his last, he said, 'Truly this man was God's Son!'" (Mark 15:39). Interestingly, this is the first time in Mark's gospel that a human being refers to Jesus as God's Son. In the opening baptismal scene and at the transfiguration, it is God who declares that Jesus is the Beloved Son, and in a third scene it is unclean spirits who shout, "You are the Son of God!" It is only at his death, then, that someone realizes that Jesus is, in fact, the Son of God. Here is a witness at the foot of the cross. Matthew even emphasizes that the centurion is "facing" Jesus. Does this mean he is seeing Jesus as he truly is? He is standing as a guard and part of the execution squad, and yet he is a witness to our salvation. Here is an unlikely disciple. His proclamation tells the truth about himself as a sinner and about the glory of God whom he sees hanging on a tree.

To be a witness means to give a testimony, to proclaim, or to announce a message. In both the Old Testament and New Testament, to give a witness is related to speaking the truth about what one has seen and what one knows. We are to "speak the truth from [our] heart" (Psalm 15:2).

In the Pentateuch there are two understandings of witness. The first has to do with law courts and the need for two witnesses to give testimony—firsthand knowledge of a fact or event—to ensure justice and fairness. The second understanding is the law against bearing false witness, speaking untruths against a neighbor.

These two meanings of bearing witness can also be found in the New Testament. Two witnesses are needed in a court of law "so that every word may be confirmed by the evidence of two or three witnesses" (Matthew 18:15-16), but there are two false witnesses at Jesus' trial, even though Jesus himself repeats the Mosaic law's injunction against bearing false witness against others.

Both the legal and moral traditions point to the essential claim on the witness: to give testimony to the truth about what they know: "Let them bring their witnesses to justify them, and let them hear and say, 'It is true'" (Isaiah 43:9).

Jesus as Witness

The New Testament writers emphasize that Jesus is a witness: a witness to the truth at his own trial and the one who is a "faithful witness, the firstborn of the dead, and the ruler of the kings of the earth" (Revelation 1:5).

Jesus calls upon his disciples to follow him as witnesses. Just as he bears witness to the Father, so he calls his disciples to be a witness to all that God has done in and through him. Luke begins and ends his gospel with the theme of witness. He writes in the opening verses that the sources of his proclamation are eyewitnesses of the life, death, and resurrection of Jesus. In the gospel's final scene, Jesus tells the disciples, "You are witnesses of these things" (Luke 24:48).

And what are they to be witnesses of? *You are witnesses,* Jesus says, *to all of this—my whole life, death, and now my resurrection. You can witness to the stories I have told, the people who were healed, the lost who were found, and the broken who were mended. You can tell people that I suffered and died, but I did it for love. You can witness to the new life I have been given by God's power to overcome sin and death.* And who should they tell and who would believe them? In the opening scene of the Acts of the Apostles, Luke's sequel to his gospel, Jesus promises to send the Spirit upon the disciples, telling them to be "my witnesses in Jerusalem, in all Judea and Samaria, and to the ends of the earth" (Acts 1:8).

We are not alone, then, in speaking the truth. The Spirit who gives birth to the church also breathes tongues of fire on each disciple. It is upon their faith that our own faith rests. Together with other disciples, the church becomes a great "cloud of witnesses" on which later generations can depend (Hebrews 12:1).

"Witness for Christ Each Day, and if Necessary Use Words"

St. Francis of Assisi allegedly said these words. Even if they are not an exact quote, it sounds like something he would say or do. His whole life was a witness to Christ, and we know that Francis would rather go out and serve the poor than stay home and write a book about service or explain it to others. His witness was embodied in his actions. Even before his conversion, Francis learned the pain of bearing witness through his actions. We know he lived the good life and loved fine things. One day when he was in the market selling his father's products, a beggar came to him asking for alms. Later, Francis ran to find him again and gave him all his money—gave him everything. But Francis was mocked by his friends and his father for his kindness. Despite their cruelty, he soon heard the call to marry "Lady Poverty."

We know that Christians should be known by their love. Who can forget the pictures of Pope John Paul II visiting the man in jail who attempted to kill him? Or Pope Francis embracing the man with neurofibromatosis, a disease in which tumors grow in the nervous system? After the images went viral, Pope Francis tweeted, "True charity requires courage: let us overcome the fear of getting our hands dirty so as to help those in need."* For St. Francis and Pope Francis, preaching the gospel begins with how we live and what we do.

But our actions are not always so transparent. It matters that our intent is truthful. When I was in high school, I went through a painful breakup with a group of close girlfriends. During my senior year, I was pretty much on my own. Instead of going to the cafeteria for lunch, I went to the chapel for Mass. My teachers and the principal thought I was a very holy kid, but I was mostly hiding out. I didn't find much solace in the Scripture or the Eucharist, and I doubted very much that God cared for my aching heart. I felt betrayed. At the end of the year, I was given an outstanding service award. But I wondered whether my teachers had misinterpreted my actions, thinking that I was more devout than I really was. They saw my service, but did they know my confused heart? Perhaps this is common for teens: we don't think people really know who we are. I came to understand, in time, that I wanted my actions to be a true witness, like that of both St. Francis and Pope Francis; I wanted what I say and what I do to speak a truth about who I am, or who I'm trying to be.

Witness Is about Words Too

Remember Dorothy Day—she gathered the poor to her table to serve them. But she also said, "If I have achieved anything in my life, . . . it is because I have not been embarrassed to talk about God."** I have been embarrassed sometimes. It is okay to talk about God at church or at the

* Pope Francis, Twitter, September 21, 2013, https://twitter.com/Pontifex/status/381317258955337728?lang=en.

** Jim Forest, "Servant of God Dorothy Day," CatholicWorker.org, February 11, 2022, https://catholicworker.org/servant-of-god-html/.

school where I'm a theologian, but I find I don't do it too quickly at a family gathering, at parties with friends, or sitting out with our neighbors. Speech about God is pretty hard these days. What if I get a mocking look?

But giving a witness is about speech. It is saying something about God and the truth of our own story. It is speech that is searching for the truth. We do not have to have all the answers lined up perfectly. We just have to tell our story about what God is doing in our lives. We just have be truthful about our joys and our doubts.

Alcoholics Anonymous is based on giving a witness. The power of this movement, which has touched millions of lives since the 1930s, has been in helping people to take the first step: saying who I am ("Hello, my name is Bill"), what I am ("I'm an alcoholic"), and telling my story ("We admitted we were powerless over alcohol—that our lives had become unmanageable.") Many people have found AA to be more authentic than going to a church. Why? Because people have to tell honest, truthful, authentic stories about their brokenness—about getting it all messed up, about falling down and not being able to get up again. Here is a community that gathers around their suffering, tells their story, and searches for God's saving help.

Sound familiar?

I Doubt That

When the disciples meet the resurrected Jesus, they are simultaneously filled with joy and disbelief. Faith and doubt, side by side. He eats for them, shows them the marks of his suffering, and allows them to see his new body. It's too good to be true. I'm not sure I can really believe all this.

And yet we are witnesses to these things. I wonder if Jesus does not mean all of it—witnessing to our joys and also to our doubts and disbeliefs. What if we were honest enough to tell each other the truth? "I'm not so sure." "I don't know where God is calling me." "I doubt God cares much." "I struggle with what is true, though I want to be sure." "Lord I believe; help my unbelief" (Mark 9:24).

Jesus knew that there would be many more disciples who would not see and yet believe. How much harder it is to believe without seeing. And yet Paul is one of those witnesses. He never saw the resurrected Christ, but he was powerfully changed by his presence.

Doubt is a part of faith. It is not opposed to faith, because doubt means that you are still in the relationship, still searching and seeking, still calling out to God for comfort, assurance, and direction. You are witnesses to all these things.

It Will Cost You

As the early Christians learned, giving a witness has consequences. Claiming to be a follower of Jesus in public can mean opposition, hardship, imprisonment, and for some, death. The word "martyr" comes from the same Greek word as "witness." The term was used for those Christians who met a violent end because of their testimony, in word and deed, but who were prepared to suffer gladly "for the name." A witness bears by testimony and a martyr by death.

Maximilian Maria Kolbe, OFM Conv, a Polish saint, was such a martyr. During World War II, his monastery chose to become a hospital. The monks saved several thousand Jews, and they continued a small publishing business. But the Nazis eventually shut them down, and Kolbe and four others were imprisoned and sent to Auschwitz. When three prisoners tried to escape, the Nazis, in an effort to deter others, chose ten men to be starved to death in an underground bunker. One of those men cried aloud, "My wife! My children!" and Kolbe volunteered to take his place. An eyewitness reported that Kolbe led the prisoners in prayer and either stood or knelt peacefully in his cell. After two weeks he was the only one alive. The Nazis then killed him by lethal injection.

Few of us are called to be martyrs. We can only hope that if the possibility arises that we must die for what we believe, then we will be ready.

Cloud of Witnesses

According to the *Catechism of the Catholic Church*, the sacrament of confirmation "gives us a special strength of the Holy Spirit to spread and defend the faith by word and action as true witnesses of Christ, to confess the name of Christ boldly, and never to be ashamed of the Cross" (no. 1316). This is the peace that Christ leaves his disciples, ensuring them that they have nothing to fear as they go forth to be his witnesses to the end of the earth, even in the face of death.

Because of the power of the Spirit, we are members of a community of witnesses. But for Catholics, giving a verbal witness is not a big part of our tradition. Evangelical Christians are great at witnessing to their faith, and in many of their churches a person gives a witness in the Sunday worship service. While our liturgy does not allow for that kind of sharing, we have found other places to hear each other's story. This is one reason why retreats such as Teens Encounter Christ or Marriage Encounter or Cursillo have become popular in our church—because people are invited to give first-person testimonies or talks. They provide a place where people come together to hear each other give a testimony about what God is doing in their lives.

But it takes practice. We need to invite others to offer their witness, and we need to have the courage ourselves to give testimony to our lives. Children and youth, as well as the elderly, can all be invited to give a witness.

Pope Francis has invited Catholics to consider the joy of evangelization. In his 2013 apostolic exhortation *Evangelii Gaudium*, he reminds us that we are witnesses to the good news: "I especially ask Christians in communities throughout the world to offer a radiant and attractive witness of fraternal communion" to others, in particular to those outside the church. "If they see the witness . . . they will find that witness luminous and attractive" (*Evangelii Gaudium*, nos. 99–100). We have to tell others about the great joy that God brings to our lives. Pope Francis ends his exhortation with a prayer to Mary (no. 288):

> Star of the new evangelization,
> help us to bear radiant witness to communion,
> service, ardent and generous faith,
> justice and love of the poor,
> that the joy of the Gospel
> may reach to the ends of the earth,
> illuminating even the fringes of our world.
>
> Mother of the living Gospel,
> wellspring of happiness for God's little ones,
> pray for us.
>
> Amen. Alleluia!

Like John the Baptist, the one who gave witness to the light, we too are called to be radiant witnesses (John 1:7).

Reflection Questions

- How can you be a witness to God's calling in your life to others in your actions and your words?
- What times of doubt have you faced and how did this impact your faith? What doubts do you carry as you consider your community, town, and region? What truth can you give witness to in this time and place?

- In your parish context, how can you invite others to tell their stories of doubt and joy, of rejection and witness?
- Recall your confirmation: what sense of calling did the sacrament have for you? How might your parish improve its confirmation program to invite youth to have the courage to give a witness with their lives?

Chapter 5

Neighbor

Laura Kelly Fanucci

He said also to the one who had invited him, "When you give a luncheon or a dinner, do not invite your friends or your brothers or your relatives or rich neighbors, in case they may invite you in return, and you would be repaid. But when you give a banquet, invite the poor, the crippled, the lame, and the blind. And you will be blessed, because they cannot repay you, for you will be repaid at the resurrection of the righteous."

Luke 14:12-14

Think of a recent party you attended or the last gathering you hosted. Who made up the guests on the invitation list? Friends, relatives, coworkers, acquaintances? You probably did not invite strangers, social outcasts, or people who are homeless or living in poverty. We tend to socialize with people we know, and we tend to return the favor by inviting others who have included us.

But once I had the opportunity to attend a party unlike any other I have ever seen. I was living in France and working in a homeless shelter with refugees from North Africa. When New Year's Eve arrived, I was shocked to find that the residents in our shelter and others in need of government assistance were invited by the town mayor to join an elegant party at the city hall. Hundreds of people from all walks of life packed the medieval banquet room. At tables set with linen tablecloths and crystal wineglasses, I sat next to men who often slept on the streets, and women who fled to our shelter seeking protection from domestic violence. We were served a five-course gourmet dinner, complete with champagne toasts and boxes of chocolates. Everyone in attendance experienced the joy of celebrating a new year with their neighbors—rich and poor, immigrant and native, young and old.

In his teaching on hospitality from Luke's gospel, Jesus turns social customs on their head in the same surprising way. Instead of keeping within comfortable circles, he calls his disciples to extend their welcome to outsiders—those who are not wealthy or healthy or able to thank us. Jesus redefines the term "neighbor" in order to teach his followers what discipleship means: that love must run wider and deeper than our instincts tell us. To follow the One who dined with tax collectors and touched lepers and welcomed prostitutes, we are called beyond family loyalty and familiar locality. We are called to see all of God's people as our neighbors.

Jesus the Neighbor

Jesus' neighbor ethic is built on the Great Commandment that unites love of God and love of neighbor. But unlike the Old Testament view of a neighbor as primarily a fellow member of the covenant community (like a sibling or kinsman), Jesus expands his teaching on neighbor to the point of embracing love for one's enemies. In Jesus' time these enemies included hated groups who were rejected as unclean or unworthy, including prostitutes, tax collectors, and lepers. Jesus welcomes such social outcasts as neighbors with whom he dines, breaking traditional laws of ritual cleanliness. Through his table fellowship, Jesus bears witness to God's expansive definition of neighbor. He invites his disciples to act as neighbors with the same radical welcome.

Jesus tackles the thorny question of "Who is my neighbor?" head-on in the parable of the Good Samaritan (Luke 10:25-37). After shocking his audience with the repulsive idea of the hated Samaritan being the source of love and goodness, Jesus asks his listeners which person in the story was a neighbor to the man who was hurt. When he receives the obvious but uncomfortable response—"The one who showed him mercy"—Jesus replies simply: "Go and do likewise."

Who Is My Neighbor?

Ultimately each of us who hears the Good Samaritan parable is put to the test with the same questions. Who is my neighbor? How do I go and do likewise? When we look to the gospels for guidance, we see how three different groups come to be included within the category of neighbor —three groups whom Jesus knew and loved in powerful ways. Neighbors are neighbors (people we know), strangers (whether near or far), and enemies (critics and opponents). By stretching our instincts past our comfort zone to include these widening circles of neighbors, strangers, and enemies, we enter into discipleship's view of "neighbor-hood" as a state of being in which all are drawn together in the household of God.

Neighbors Are Neighbors

When I look around my own neighborhood, I'm reminded of how important neighbors can be. One neighbor pulls our trashcan back to the house when we're gone on vacation. Another neighbor plows our driveway after overnight snowstorms. One family brought us a meal after my surgery. Another couple surprised us with a gift after our son was born. Communities are strengthened when we treat our neighbors well. This social bond allows us to join together when things go wrong.

Years ago I was driving down my street when I saw a couple out for their morning walk, a routine that always brought them by our house, where they would stop and chat about their grandchildren or local news. But that day, I noticed something was wrong. Instead of their normal pace, the husband was leaning into his wife at a strange angle as they shuffled slowly down the street. I pulled over to ask what was wrong, and she gasped that he was having a diabetic attack and could barely speak or walk. I told them to wait there, put my car in reverse, and floored back down the street to grab a carton of orange juice from our refrigerator. After several minutes of sitting together by the side of the road while we helped the man take small sips of juice, he slowly started to regain his normal look and composure. Later I walked with them back to their home, and along the way the wife said how grateful she was that our paths crossed at that moment. She did not know many neighbors along our street, so she was not sure what she would have done if I had not driven by and recognized that something was wrong.

Our neighbors include people we know. They may be family, friends, colleagues at work, or members of the communities in which we live and work. This is the most common understanding of "neighbor": someone who shares something with us, whether a ZIP code, a back alley, or membership in a group. We often define neighbors based on similarity: same school district, same bus stop, or same grocery store. Although we have different levels of intimacy with our neighbors—some are friends with whom we enjoy backyard barbecues; some are acquaintances to whom we wave while walking the dog—we are accustomed to this idea of neighbors from our earliest childhood memories of playing with neighborhood kids or longing for friends who lived right down the road.

Neighbors of the ordinary kind can still be challenging to accept, however. We know it is often hardest to love those who are closest to us: spouses, children, parents, or roommates. Living near each other means that we have to put up with each other's faults, failings, and annoying habits day after day. But these relationships can also become sources of mutual love. Jesus knew this truth through caring for his own relatives and friends. But he did so with a radical love that invited those close to him to reconsider their relationships in light of the wideness of God's mercy.

Mark's gospel describes Jesus' surprising response when his own family calls out to him while he is teaching in the middle of a crowd: "And looking at those who sat around him, he said, 'Here are my mother and brothers! Whoever does the will of God is my brother and sister and mother'" (Mark 3:31-35). This unexpected message must have been challenging for Jesus' family and friends to hear. But he wanted the people he loved to start seeing the world through changed eyes. Eyes that saw who God was loving and called them to love too.

Neighbors Are Strangers

While on his evening watch as a solider, St. Martin of Tours saw a beggar shivering in the winter cold by the city gate. He drew his sword, cut his cloak in two, and offered half to the poor man to keep him warm. That night, Martin dreamed he saw Jesus wearing that same cloak—a startling and stark reminder of finding Christ in the face of the poor. Because of his strange dream, Martin decided to give up his military service and embrace a radical call to Christian pacifism. As Jesus' teachings on banquet hospitality from Luke's gospel remind us, disciples are called to extend generous invitations toward our neighbors—not to those who can repay us, but to those who will never invite us in return, write a kind thank-you note, or even smile in appreciation.

To be a neighbor in the terms of Christian discipleship is to answer a call to stretch, to push beyond what feels comfortable, and to live in the tension of what is unknown, even when love or service may be inconvenient. While we would be happy to define neighbor by location (proximity) or relationship (closeness), Jesus asks us to take a further step and redefine the relationship based on our common kinship as God's children. The fact that someone simply lives, regardless of where or how they live, makes them our neighbor because all are God's beloved.

While society's definition of neighbor may keep us divided by income, race, religion, political party, or even our beloved sports teams, the kinship of the reign of God bursts apart these boundaries. Discipleship demands that we learn to love those who are different from us, without expecting to be loved in return. So our neighbors must include strangers, whether people in our own communities whom we do not know or those who are geographically distant from us.

In recent decades, the United States bishops have issued strong calls for Catholics to consider how they extend a compassionate welcome to immigrants in their communities. If the stranger is to be welcomed as Christ, then we must examine how our attitude toward the unknown reflects our faith in God, who often appears in surprising disguise. Do we greet the stranger at our door with the best we have to offer, as Abraham did when the three men arrived at his tent with surprising news? Or do we hold back out of fear, misunderstanding, judgment, or selfishness?

Being a good neighbor is not simply about caring for those who look, think, believe, or act like we do. Even though the sinful realities of racism and prejudice run deep, we believe as Christians that love runs even deeper. We can commit ourselves to retrain our instincts and learn not to judge strangers by their appearance or circumstances. We can let Christ's generous hospitality reshape our hearts and remind us how the Christian life is given in service to those in need, whether or not we know or like them.

Neighbors Are Enemies

Jesus' final redefinition of neighbor is the ultimate, the unthinkable, the greatest test of our discipleship: to embrace our enemies, to welcome our critics, and to forgive those who hurt us. We are not often faced with someone seeking to take our life or inflict physical harm. But if we are honest with ourselves, it is not hard to think up a lesser enemy or two. Maybe an estranged relative against whom we hold a grudge, a former friendship whose bridges have been burned, or a business relationship that has turned sour.

Enemies in Jesus' time were often communally defined by tribal rivalries, similar to the way we think about enemies today in terms of nations at war. But our personal enemies may come from traumas, like divorce or being fired from a job. When relationships are ruptured, we feel betrayed and wounded. The idea of forgiving the one who caused us deep pain—let alone learning to love them as our neighbor—can seem outrageous.

Indeed, it is a natural response to call someone our enemy when they cause us harm. But Jesus' radical forgiveness for those who hated him invites us to reframe our situations. While Jesus never sanctions any action of evil, violence, or abuse, he invites his disciples to release the resentment in their hearts so that their lives are not poisoned by hatred and bitterness. By turning adversaries into neighbors, we can experience powerful freedom.

Recently I witnessed the healing of a relationship between two relatives who had become enemies. For several years they had refused to socialize at family functions. They even refused to speak to each other if their paths crossed. What had started as a misunderstanding involving money grew into a fierce grudge, impacting both of their families. Gradually, though, the hatred between them began to subside, bearing truth to the saying that keeping a grudge is hard work.

As I watched the two begin to speak and visit with each other again, despite all the hurt that their fight had caused them, I remembered times in my own life when I needed a massage to heal deep knots in my neck and shoulders. It is extremely painful for long-held tensions to be worked out. Even afterward, when we expect the healing to bring release, there can still be soreness and lingering tenderness. But this pain is a different kind of ache. It affirms that we have been carrying around a heavy burden and need to make changes so we don't fall back into bad habits. Learning to live as neighbors with those who are not easy to love is not about reciprocity or repayment. Faithful discipleship is imitating the One who asks us to love our enemies.

Here Comes Everybody

My mother-in-law has a gift for hospitality. She loves to host family gatherings and welcome friends into her home. But she also goes a step beyond and extends a welcome to complete strangers. She invites anyone who does not have a place to spend a holiday to join our family, and she even rearranges the dining room to make one long table so that everyone feels included. Over the years I have passed plates to new neighbors from Egypt, distant relatives from

Canada, families from Colombia, and seminary students from Nigeria. She sends strangers home with heaping plates of leftovers, and she often ends up inviting them to join her for a weekend at the family cabin. My mother-in-law has taught me much about being a neighbor as a practice of Christian discipleship: how it is a generous welcome and a habit of hospitality that always makes room at the table for someone hungry for food or friendship.

For those called to the vocation of marriage, giving oneself to a spouse for life means a radical redefinition of being neighbors, too. We are no longer connected only to our family of origin, but to a spouse who invites us into a new constellation of relationships—in-laws, extended relatives, friends, and coworkers. As partners who pledge our lives to each other with sacred vows, we are called to be neighbors to all of those whom our spouse brings into our life, even if we don't like them. Marriage is an extended exercise in neighborliness. Our spouse becomes our closest neighbor, living side by side day after day. They call us in turn to accept those who were formerly strangers as our kin, and they even challenge us to learn how to love difficult people we might prefer to write off as enemies. The book of Ruth offers a powerful story about a daughter and mother-in-law who were once strangers from different groups and now cling together after tragedy strikes. Ruth commits herself to Naomi, saying: "Where you go, I will go; where you lodge, I will lodge; your people shall be my people, and your God my God" (Ruth 1:16).

The whole family of the church gathers each time we celebrate the Eucharist, the sacrament that broadens our vision of who is our neighbor. This ritual meal in which sinners and strangers join to break bread echoes Jesus' table fellowship with tax collectors, prostitutes, and social outcasts. We are called to gather with those who may seem outwardly our opposites, because they too are our brothers and sisters in Christ.

We also practice being neighbors through the prayers of the faithful, which gather our concerns as a community. We pray together for our church, our nation and world, global and local leaders, community and international tragedies, the poor and lonely, the sick and dying, and our beloved deceased, who remain our neighbors even in death. This is the definition of the Body of Christ: all who are connected as children of God.

The call to be neighbors reminds us that the demands of discipleship are not chosen according to our preferences or our control. This calling to love both God and neighbor will always be lived out within a sinful world where we cross paths and jostle elbows with people whom we do not like. But we are still called to love them with a Christlike love, whether intimate friend or mortal enemy.

This call to "neighbor-hood" transforms us. We are not left unchanged by these encounters or the effort it takes to continue loving in concrete deeds and words each new day.

Reflection Questions

- Picture the first person who comes to mind when you hear the word "neighbor." Why did you pick this person? How have they influenced the way you think about being a neighbor? How has your understanding of what it means to be a neighbor been impacted by the COVID-19 pandemic or other challenging events of recent years?
- Now picture someone who comes to mind when you hear the word "enemy." Why did you pick this person? Who is an enemy in the groups you belong to—your family, friends, parish, town, country? How might God be calling you to show love toward an enemy?

- When have you acted as a neighbor to someone who lives near you? To a stranger? To someone whom you struggle to love?
- When did someone who is a stranger or an enemy reach out to you as a neighbor?
- Next time you participate in Mass, pay close attention to the prayers of the faithful. Which petition can you carry with you for the next week, to practice being a neighbor through your prayer?
- Read the US bishops' pastoral letter on immigration, "Welcoming the Stranger Among Us: Unity in Diversity" (available online from www.usccb.org). In what ways does your parish or community welcome immigrants, or not? What more could your community do to learn about current immigration issues and policies? If there are recent immigrants in your area, how might you invite them to share their stories with you?

Chapter 6

Forgiver

Kathleen A. Cahalan

One of the Pharisees asked Jesus to eat with him, and he went into the Pharisee's house and took his place at the table. And a woman in the city, who was a sinner, having learned that he was eating in the Pharisee's house, brought an alabaster jar of ointment. She stood behind him at his feet, weeping, and began to bathe his feet with her tears and to dry them with her hair. Then she continued kissing his feet and anointing them with the ointment. Now when the Pharisee who had invited him saw it, he said to himself, "If this man were a prophet, he would have known who and what kind of woman this is who is touching him—that she is a sinner." Jesus spoke up and said to him, "Simon, I have something to say to you." "Teacher," he replied, "speak." "A certain creditor had two debtors; one owed five hundred denarii, and the other fifty. When they could not pay, he canceled the debts for both of them. Now which of them will love him more?" Simon answered, "I suppose the one for whom he canceled the greater debt." And Jesus said to him, "You have judged rightly." Then turning toward the woman, he said to Simon, "Do you see this woman? I entered your house; you gave me no water for my feet, but she has bathed my feet with her tears and dried them with her hair. You gave me no kiss, but from the time I came in she has not stopped kissing my feet. You did not anoint my head with oil, but she has anointed my feet with ointment. Therefore, I tell you, her sins, which were many, have been forgiven; hence she has shown great love. But the one to whom little is forgiven, loves little." Then he said to her, "Your sins are forgiven." But those who were at the table with him began to say among themselves, "Who is this who even forgives sins?" And he said to the woman, "Your faith has saved you; go in peace."

Luke 7:36-50

Seeking Forgiveness

St. Jane Frances de Chantal lost her beloved husband in a hunting accident. As he was dying, he forgave the man who shot him and told him, "Don't commit the sin of hating yourself when you have done nothing wrong." Jane did not feel the same as her husband. She could not forgive the man who took her husband's life. As a good Christian, however, she tried to be nice to him when she saw him. Over time, though, she felt called to invite him to her home. With more time and opportunities to know him, she was able to forgive him. Eventually she became the godmother of his child. I'm comforted to know that forgiving another can take a long time.

My sins are smaller and perhaps more trivial, but they can do great harm. Just last week, I lit some candles before our company came for dinner, and my husband warned me that the wax could drip onto our beautiful runner, so I should put something beneath them. I did not heed his warning, one he has given several times. When the candles did drip, my husband was furious. As the doorbell was ringing I quickly replaced them. During dinner I noticed the replacements were making a worse mess. Not once, but twice I made the same mistake. I could clean up the candle wax, but asking forgiveness—saying "I'm sorry I didn't listen to you"—is much harder. Marriages are built on forgiving one another, and they can be destroyed by failing to practice forgiveness.

Being Forgiven

Luke recounts the story of "the pardoned woman," but it should really be called "the pardoned woman and the unpardoned Pharisee." The story is filled with juxtapositions: man and woman, named and unnamed, rich and poor, the one who knows the law and the one outside the law, the invited guests and the party-crasher. They are paired as opposites, one higher and one lower on the social scale. But by the end of the story, a complete reversal has occurred, which is one of Luke's favorite insights about discipleship.

Simon welcomes Jesus, a popular teacher, to his table, but is shocked that Jesus lets an unclean, sinful woman touch him. Simon is concerned that nothing upset his evening, for he has set his table with lavish food and drink and invited all the "right" people. And yet he misses the point of hospitality, as Jesus points out. Simon has failed to offer water for cleaning Jesus' feet (a common custom in a dusty environment), a kiss of welcome (another common custom of greeting), and anointing his head with oil (not a common custom for a guest but an important ritual for Israel's kings as well as their dead). Luke has moved the story of Jesus' anointing for his burial—which Mark and Matthew tell prior to the Last Supper—to the beginning of Jesus' ministry in order to point to Jesus' true identity: the anointed Messiah who will die. But Simon clearly does not understand who Jesus is. Simon recognizes Jesus as a prophet but questions his judgment. Does Jesus not know that this woman is a sinner and that he should not be touched by her if he is to remain clean? Simon misses the point that Jesus is not only prophet but Messiah, Savior, and King.

There is a good bit of irony and humor here. Jesus knows that Simon is judging the woman and has failed to see her or the love that she has shown. So he engages Simon in a bit of Socratic dialogue, asking him to identify who has greater love, the one forgiven a great debt or a small debt. Of course, Simon knows the person with the greater debt would love more. Then comes the punch line: Simon, "you have judged rightly!" But of course we know he has judged her wrongly.

Do we see this woman? She is Luke's favorite gospel character: she is poor and lowly, a sinner and an outcast. Yet what lavish love she shows to Jesus. Her treasure is her love. But it creates incredible disorder, for she has upset the dinner party. In another clever juxtaposition, she becomes the prophet by upsetting the balance of power and demonstrating a radical display of love. She is also a foot-washer, reminiscent of John's gospel image of service at the Last Supper. And she, a woman, is anointing the king of Israel. Now *that* is role reversal.

Regardless of roles, she and Simon are both sinners. Yet it is not their sins that distinguish them. Her sins are many, whatever they are, but she has repented. She seeks to serve Jesus in humility, and she acknowledges him as king and savior. She judges rightly.

Called to Be Forgiven

Learning to be a forgiver begins with first recognizing that I am a sinner and that my actions hurt other people. I have to start with seeking forgiveness. When I am forgiven, then I know love and I can learn to practice forgiving others. Forgiving others for their sins against me requires great love.

The sacrament of reconciliation shows us the way to follow. It begins with contrition. When I've sinned against another, I cannot seek their forgiveness without truly feeling sorry for what I have done. I must be able to recognize that when I harmed another, showed disrespect, hurt their feelings, and damaged our relationship, I may be untrustworthy in their eyes. I knew the minute I saw the dripping candle wax that I had done wrong, and I felt terrible. In asking forgiveness, I needed to show that I really felt sorry about not heeding the warning. Seeking forgiveness is about taking the steps to restore that trust. And it begins with feeling my own sorrow at what I have done. Contrition is the desire to be free from the burden of sin and guilt.

Once I recognize my wrongdoing, I have to muster up the courage to admit it, to say "I'm sorry." I must witness against myself. This can be hard, even humiliating, in front of another. To confess is to speak aloud the words, to tell another that I have done wrong.

But, of course, words can be empty if they are not heartfelt and followed by a change in behavior. We can sense when someone is not really sorry for what they have done. I must change my ways to build up the trust in the relationship again. I must show the person I offended that I will not do it again. After cleaning up that runner, I put some discs below the candle sticks to catch any wax in the future.

In saying "I'm sorry" to another, I must be willing to take responsibility and bear their pain, even if I do not understand it completely. What is important is that I recognize that I have harmed a child of God. I repent the sin, I admit I was wrong, and I ask for forgiveness. Then I wait and accept what happens, for it is up to the person I have harmed to forgive me or not. I counted on my husband's forgiveness because much love has come from forgiving each other in big and small ways.

The sacrament of reconciliation is built on these steps, and its goal is to restore our relationship to God and to each other. But it can't be treated as cheap grace. Sometimes I rush to forgive another because I don't want conflict and pain. But then I feel resentful. Or I go to the sacrament of reconciliation, but I still feel bad about what I've done. It is normal to have these feelings. What the sacrament proclaims is that God forgives us and God helps us practice forgiveness with each other.

God's Forgiveness

The Israelites came to understand over the course of their relationship with Yahweh that their sins separated them from the divine covenant, but the covenant could be restored through repentance, atonement, and seeking Yahweh's forgiveness. The Israelite community developed rituals of atonement and sacrifice through burnt offerings that expressed the destruction of their sin. Animal sacrifice symbolized a "guilt-offering" through which sins were confessed and the priest declared, "You shall be forgiven." In addition to rituals, Moses begged God to forgive the people's sins and restore the bonds of the covenant: "Forgive the iniquity of this people according to the greatness of your steadfast love" (Numbers 14:19).

Old Testament authors were not afraid to reveal the reality of unforgiveness and the desire to not forgive. The psalmist hurls bitterness toward his and God's enemies: "If only you would kill the wicked, O God!" (Psalm 139:19). The prophets tell God to *not* forgive the sinner. Jeremiah repeats a similar refrain: "Do not forgive their iniquity, do not blot out their sin from your sight" (Jeremiah 18:23). But in that struggle to understand divine forgiveness, the prophets also proclaim God's perspective on forgiveness: "I will cleanse them from all the guilt of their sin against me, and I will forgive all the guilt of their sin and rebellion against me" (Jeremiah 33:8).

What we must learn is that God's forgiveness does not make sense. A follower can never gain forgiveness or equality with God through reparation or ritual sacrifice: "For you have no delight in sacrifice; if I were to give a burnt offering, you would not be pleased" (Psalm 51:16). Rather, a "broken and contrite heart" is the sign that the follower knows their sin and lack of love and seeks to be in communion with Yahweh again. The prophets had to learn that God forgives because God loves: "I will love them freely, for my anger has turned from them" (Hosea 14:4).

On our own, we cannot free ourselves from our wrongdoings or forgive the wrongs we endure. Being a forgiver is not about greater personal effort or just trying harder. We can practice forgiveness because we realize that God's love conquers all our sins, a love that empowers disciples to seek and grant forgiveness. Neighbor love precedes and follows forgiveness in the Christian story. We can forgive because we've been shown great love.

Forgiving Another

If we want to be a forgiver, the practice is basically the same as seeking forgiveness. First, we must feel the anger, the sorrow, the hurt, and the pain. Usually the inability to grasp the emotion of being offended by another is reason enough for not walking down the path of forgiveness. If we can feel the emotions deeply, we can decide what to do about them. Do we want to hang on to the bitterness we feel, or do we want to be free from it? We have a choice. It does not mean forgetting or excusing the wrong. It means admitting that this happened, recognizing its pain, but seeking to be free from it.

The next step is to change the way we view the person who has harmed us. We can step back and try to see them as a person who is broken and a sinner and who is deserving of love and compassion. We judge the act and let go of hating the person. If we can follow through to this point, we find some peace and hope. We can experience a new freedom.

Wait, you might be thinking, *that sounds way too easy*. But it is important to remember that we can forgive another person for what they have done to us. It does not mean we have to reconcile the relationship. Reconciliation, the healing between two people, comes after forgiveness.

Jesus as Forgiver

There is another story in Luke's gospel about a pair of sinners. Two thieves are crucified alongside Jesus, one on the right and one on the left. Jesus is the innocent one, and the thieves are both guilty. One tells him to get them out of this mess: "Are you not the Messiah? Save yourself and us!" But the other sinner responds differently. Like the pardoned woman, this sinner acknowledges his sinfulness and need for Christ's redemption: "We indeed have been condemned justly, for we are getting what we deserve for our deeds, but this man has done nothing wrong. Jesus, remember me when you come into your kingdom" (Luke 23:39, 41-42). Clearly this sinner knows his savior and king.

The world is divided not between good and bad people, but between the unrepentant and the repentant. All of us are sinners—the Pharisee and the woman, the thief on the right and the thief on the left. On the one side are those people who are busy identifying the sins of others and judging them harshly, and on the other side are those who have recognized their own sin and seek forgiveness.

Jesus embodies forgiveness and shows us how to be a forgiver. Because Yahweh loves, Yahweh forgives. We are loved, and so we can forgive. When we forgive, we renew the bonds of love. Divine and human reconciliation are caught up with each other. Unless we forgive a neighbor a wrong, God will not forgive our wrongs, and unless we seek God's forgiveness for our sins, we have little capacity to become forgivers: "For if you forgive others their trespasses, your heavenly Father will also forgive you; but if you do not forgive others, neither will your Father forgive your trespasses" (Matthew 6:14-15).

Jesus preaches a radical gospel of divine love and forgiveness. Forgiveness is God's very nature and purpose, for through it God shows the immensity of love. To those who do not observe the ritual law, to the outcast and the sick, to those who have done wrong, Jesus proclaims, "Friend, your sins are forgiven you" (Luke 5:20). And to the thief, he offers forgiveness at the moment they are both about to die: "Truly I tell you, today you will be with me in Paradise" (Luke 23:43).

This is not always good news, however. Some people could not accept Jesus' view of divine forgiveness and love. Jesus tries to make the teaching on forgiveness easier to practice: "Do not judge, and you will not be judged; do not condemn, and you will not be condemned. Forgive, and you will be forgiven" (Luke 6:37). Yet even that simplified teaching is rejected.

Simon is right: Jesus is a prophet, and he is condemned because of blasphemy about forgiveness of sins. His own suffering and execution, as an innocent person in the face of false charges, brings Jesus to a place of abandonment, loneliness, and pain. And yet Jesus' love for God and his followers led him to a radical step of obedience, to lay down his life for his friends, and to offer forgiveness to those who crucify him.

That's the path of discipleship.

Forgiving the Worst Sins

Being a forgiver is a difficult path to follow, both in seeking forgiveness and in granting it. Many of the wounds people bear from violence, murder, war, torture, or rape are so horrible that it takes years for them to find comfort, healing, and reconciliation. Our own church is living through the pain of recognizing how much abuse and deceit has happened at the hands of our leaders. Too many lives are broken by this sin—trust destroyed, communities damaged, and lives mangled. Just hearing one person's story of being abused brings me so much sorrow and pain and anger. Hearing some of the stories of abusers also makes me sad, for many were themselves victims of great abuse. I can hardly wrap my head and heart around all that damage. I don't know how to forgive all this.

Because disciples understand their call as members of the Body of Christ, it seems hard to accept that the very relationships that are meant to give life and companionship are often the source of our greatest pain and suffering. Forgiveness is not a simple matter in human relationships. Most often, it is a process that takes time, healing, and the help of others. We must be patient and not rush to premature forgiveness or refuse to ever forgive. We cannot love with a hardened heart. But we can pray the words Jesus said on the cross: "Father, forgive them" (Luke 23:34).

On Ash Wednesday, churches are packed full. Perhaps it is because we need to gather as a community of sinners and hear the call to be a forgiver. And when we can't forgive completely, we can ask God to forgive those who have hurt us and be patient with us while we try to catch up to God's divine love.

Start Small

We have to practice being a forgiver in small ways. Those candle sticks? We all know the story is not about dripping wax. It's about not respecting what my husband asked. I think our marriages would be stronger and more loving if we learned the art of forgiveness—of asking to be forgiven and offering each other forgiveness. Perhaps each year when we set a beautiful table to celebrate our wedding anniversary, we could also incorporate the practice of forgiveness: saying "I'm sorry" for all that I have done to hurt you, and forgiving you for what you have done to hurt me. Now that would be a love feast.

Reflection Questions

- What do you fear in offering forgiveness to someone who hurt you?
- How am I called to be a forgiver? Whom do I need to forgive? How might telling that story help me to find some peace? Is there a trauma that has happened to you that seems impossible to forgive? What's a small step you might take to begin the journey?
- To whom do I need to say I am sorry? What can give me the courage to tell the truth about my sorrow and desire for forgiveness?
- In addition to the sacrament of reconciliation, how can I seek God's gracious love to forgive all my sins so that I can be a person of great love and know Christ's peace?
- What are some small steps to practice forgiveness? How might we celebrate anniversaries or birthdays or other holidays by incorporating practices of forgiveness?
- How can our communities heal and forgive in the face of violence, hatred, and injustice? What is one concrete way in which your parish or local community could work toward reconciliation between different groups in conflict with each other?

Chapter 7

Prophet

Laura Kelly Fanucci

When he entered Jerusalem, the whole city was in turmoil, asking, "Who is this?" The crowds were saying, "This is the prophet Jesus from Nazareth in Galilee."

Then Jesus entered the temple and drove out all who were selling and buying in the temple, and he overturned the tables of the money changers and the seats of those who sold doves. He said to them, "It is written,

'My house shall be called a house of prayer';
but you are making it a den of robbers."

The blind and the lame came to him in the temple, and he cured them.

Matthew 21:10-14

You probably did not turn to this chapter first.

Prophet is not a calling we go seeking. Even the biblical prophets who were called by God often ran from what was asked of them, like Jonah fleeing by ship. Most of us did not grow up wanting to become a radical truth teller, calling God's people back to justice and faithfulness in a world gone wrong. We picture extraordinary prophets from history or Scripture, and we may think that our own ordinary lives have little to do with their work.

But acting prophetically is at the heart of what it means to follow Christ. Our callings are not always easy affirmations of what we want to do with our lives. They can be edgy and uncomfortable. Yet the courage to speak the truth also comes from God, and we can trust that God stands by his prophets.

Jesus as Prophet

Jesus begins his public ministry by proclaiming the words of the prophet Isaiah within his synagogue, to the astonishment—and even anger—of those who had known him only as Joseph's son. Much like his cousin John the Baptist and many prophets of Israel before him, Jesus calls people to repentance by warning against empty religious practices and injustices toward the poor and marginalized. Jesus invites people to return to right relationship with God, who is loving and merciful. Sometimes Jesus' prophetic words and actions were dramatic, as when he overturned the tables of the moneychangers and drove sellers out of the temple. Sometimes his prophetic work was quieter, as when he cured the blind and lame who came seeking him.

But unlike Israel's prophets who preached about the evil of their people's ways and their hope that a new king and a new nation would be established, Jesus preached a new kind of good news. He preached the coming of the reign of God not as a physical place or a new era in Israel's history, but as a radically different way of encountering God active in human history: freeing the oppressed, seeking the lost, forgiving the sinner, healing the sick, comforting the grieving, and offering new life to the dying.

Jesus' prophetic message is that nothing stands in the way of God's love. No sin, social status, or situation can block God's mercy. While the promise of peace and justice that Jesus preached was consistent with Israel's covenant tradition, his message still shocked many who heard it and wanted another kind of kingdom—an earthly, political power. They heard Jesus' claims about God as blasphemous, and they ultimately sought to take his life for his prophetic, challenging words.

Yet after Jesus' resurrection, the early church still did not shy away from prophecy. Paul named prophecy as one of the gifts of the Spirit and encouraged early Christian communities to practice prophecy as part of their worship. Paul believed that the call to speak prophetically was an essential part of what it means to follow Christ, and that this call was not simply about condemnation, but consolation. He encouraged Christians to speak truth to one another in order to build up their communities: "those who prophesy speak to other people for their upbuilding and encouragement and consolation" (1 Corinthians 14:3). Just as Jesus comforted more than he condemned, Paul taught that prophecy is how Christians build up the church.

Our Turn

So how do we live and act as prophets in the world today? We mistake the prophet's role when we think that prophecy is limited to a magical prediction of future events or a frightening figure preaching doom and gloom on the street corner. To be a prophet is instead to see what is wrong, broken, missing, or unjust in our society and to speak a word of truth that shines light on the situation. Rather than pointing a finger at other groups, prophets speak to their own people, calling the community around them to return to right relationship with each other and with God. This is what makes a prophet's work challenging yet compelling: their truth is spoken directly to those they know and love.

Prophets see a wider reality than what is immediately present. They hold strong convictions driven by faithful imagination: that neighborhoods should be free from violence, that all families should have healthy food on their tables, that the natural world should be protected, that voices of people on society's margins should be heard, that life should be respected at all stages, and that workers should be paid a living wage. Prophets are not only the few bold leaders who make headlines. They are also parents who work to make schools safe and accessible for children with special needs. They are amateur athletes who raise awareness for diseases by raising funds at local races. They are grassroots organizers who hold vigil outside abortion clinics or state executions. Prophets see what is and know that it could be—and should be—more.

And the good news is that prophets can be ordinary and extraordinary, young and old, individuals and communities —all of us.

Extraordinary and Ordinary

Prophets see the world as God sees the world and seek to share this vision with others. But their methods and messages can vary. Some prophets are dramatic and extraordinary. They make the nightly news with their protests or spearhead large movements of activists. John the Baptist was a prophetic figure who emerged from the wilderness to prepare people for Jesus' coming, crying out for repentance and baptizing for the forgiveness of sins, "clothed with camel's hair, with a leather belt around his waist, and he ate locusts and wild honey" (Mark 1:6). Joan of Arc was another intense prophet from the church's history: a peasant girl who heard angelic voices telling her to lead the French in their war against the English. Her political involvement, inspired by deep faith, ultimately led to her being burned at the stake. Both John the Baptist and Joan of Arc have captured the church's imagination throughout the centuries, evident in paintings and other works of art, as Christians found hope in these symbols of powerful faith and commitment.

Yet other prophets are quiet and unassuming in their work. In my hometown in Michigan, a local veteran has earned the nickname "Flagman" for his practice of running while carrying the POW/MIA flag to honor those who did not return home from their service in Vietnam. I often see him jogging down the street when I visit my parents, and I am always grateful for this reminder of sacrifice that keeps alive the memory of the soldiers with whom he served. But the more I learned about his story, the more I was struck by his commitment. He is running one mile for every American who was killed or listed as a prisoner of war or missing in action in Vietnam—over fifty-eight thousand miles since he started this practice more than thirty years ago. Carrying a flag might seem like a small step, but the symbolism of his action has a powerful impact in his community. He transformed his ordinary exercise routine into a prophetic witness.

Young and Old

The invitation to be a prophet is not waiting for us once we have achieved maturity. Disciples are called to be prophets from our earliest days. Baptism initiates us into a faith that stands in sharp contrast to popular culture. Even as children, we are asked to speak up for what is right. The moral formation that parents give—teaching children to do the right thing even when it is unpopular—is an initiation into what it means to be a prophet. Indeed, youth can sometimes feel the freest to be prophetic and unfettered by adulthood's social pressures to conform to the status quo and accept the injustices that have always been.

When my sister was seventeen years old, she entered a local pageant for St. Patrick's Day sponsored by an area association of Irish Catholics. What was normally a cheerful celebration of Irish Americans' favorite holiday took a prophetic twist when she stepped to the podium. Instead of singing "Danny Boy" or performing Irish step dancing as other contestants did each year, she began by saying, "I wish to speak a word about Northern Ireland." Her speech on the political conflict between Catholics and Protestants might have seemed more controversial than the performances of her peers, but she wanted to speak up about a situation and a people for whom she cared deeply. The judges were so impressed by her powerful words that she won the contest. Communities of all kinds, including parishes, need the prophetic eyes and energy of youth to remember what is unjust about our world and how we are called to be the change that can transform society.

Elders can be prophetic truth-tellers too. Like youth, they are not bound by social niceties or concerned about ruffling feathers. Older adults can often speak their minds freely because they are firmly grounded in their sense of self, their core beliefs, and their view of a world they have watched change around them. Many of us have experienced this truth-telling among older relatives who are unafraid to share their hard-earned wisdom (often around the holiday table at family gatherings!).

The Gospel of Luke tells the story of two elders—Simeon and Anna—who greeted Mary and Joseph with prophetic words when they presented Jesus in the temple. Each of these prophets gave years of their lives looking toward the redemption of Israel, and finally they could see the truth of what God will do through Jesus: "Simeon took him in his arms and praised God, saying, 'Master, now you are dismissing your servant in peace, according to your word; for my eyes have seen your salvation, which you have prepared in the presence of all peoples, a light for revelation to the Gentiles and for glory to your people Israel" (Luke

2:28-32). Likewise Anna finds renewed energy and hope in what she believes God is doing through Jesus: "At that moment she came, and began to praise God and to speak about the child to all who were looking for the redemption of Jerusalem" (2:38). Despite being advanced in years, Anna and Simeon have clear eyes to see how God is at work in the world. They cannot help sharing this truth with all who will listen. From our earliest days until our last, we are given opportunities to speak prophetically about signs of hope and God's liberating justice.

Individuals and Communities

Many Catholics grew up praying the Hail Mary or reciting the *Magnificat*. Yet we can overlook the prophetic power of Mary's words in the story of her visit to Elizabeth. In response to her relative's joyful greeting, Mary offers her own song of praise to the God of justice: "He has brought down the powerful from their thrones, and lifted up the lowly; he has filled the hungry with good things, and sent the rich away empty" (Luke 1:52-54). Mary was a humble peasant girl, but her prophetic words have echoed down through the centuries for innumerable Christians. Our efforts at prophetic discipleship can do the same. They start small but grow into something bigger than our own dreams as we work together for the reign of God.

Sometimes the words and actions of a single person can ripple outward to have a huge impact. For several years, I belonged to a small-town parish in a community with many farms and greenhouses. Every year seasonal workers would come up from Mexico to work with planting, tending, and harvesting the summer and fall crops. The deacon in our parish became concerned about the treatment of these immigrant workers. They were often denied water or food breaks and lacked adequate housing. Inspired by the US

Catholic bishops' teaching on immigration, our deacon became a passionate advocate for immigrants in our area. He saw them as brothers and sisters in Christ, regardless of their legal status, and he mobilized grassroots efforts among parishioners to provide food and clothing for those in need. I remember him speaking passionately at a meeting of our parish social justice committee about our call to welcome the strangers in our midst. "If this means I wind up in jail, I'm fully prepared to do so," he said over and over. "This is doing the work of the gospel."

Communities are also called to be prophetic, inspiring individuals in turn. Each year the ritual of washing feet at the Holy Thursday Mass of the Lord's Supper offers an example of a communal prophetic action. When we bend low to wash each other's feet, we are reminded that we are part of a community that seeks to serve others and love as we have been loved by God. This gesture symbolizes our calling as disciples sent forth into the world to love in radical, prophetic ways—even kneeling at each other's feet.

"Prophets of a Future Not Our Own"

The anointing of the sick stands as a testimony to what we believe about life and death as Christians. When we anoint the sick, we set their suffering in the light of Christ's own dying and rising to new life. We embrace their pain, which is a countercultural act in a society that prefers to push people to the margins when their bodies are no longer healthy or beautiful. We literally touch the brokenness of the sick as the priest anoints their hands and head with sacred chrism oil, another prophetic symbol in a culture that has degraded and sexualized the act of human touch. We pray words of healing and hope, even when the person is gravely ill or at time of death. What could be more prophetic than to believe in God's saving power even when all signs point to the opposite?

The anointing of the sick stands as a striking witness to what our church believes about the healing power of God's grace, even when bodily health is not restored. This same truth was seen in the life and death of Pope St. John Paul II, who suffered from Parkinson's disease. The world watched him decline physically, but he refused to hide his suffering. Even when he could only speak a few words at a time, his presence spoke volumes about the value of human life up until its end. Knowing that we belong to a community that is unafraid to see suffering and lift up those in greatest need is a powerful, prophetic reminder to all of us in our times of struggle.

Ideally, our parishes will be sources of support and companionship that carry us through the burnout or discouragement that can accompany prophetic work. Just as Jesus regularly retreated from his active ministry to pray and submit his life to the will of God, so can our prayer and celebration of the sacraments sustain our prophetic efforts. We are reminded to place our own work within the wider reign of God, which is already breaking into our midst.

Taking the long view reminds us that whatever contribution we can make is part of the prophetic work of the church. But it is not up to us to save a world that has already been redeemed by Christ. A popular reflection often attributed to St. Oscar Romero (but actually penned by Bishop Kenneth Untener of Saginaw, Michigan) reminds us of this truth: "We may never see the end results, but that is the difference between the master builder and the worker. We are workers, not master builders; ministers, not messiahs. We are prophets of a future not our own."

Practicing humility as part of our prophetic discipleship grounds us in our shared humanity. Especially in the digital age, when we are bombarded with news of suffering around the globe, we can find perspective in the Body of Christ: none of us is called to do or to be all that the world needs. Our call is to do our prophetic part and to support others in their own. Humility is the foundation of faithfulness, remembering that we are flawed but still graced to do good in the world. Ultimately, the future belongs to God.

When Jesus first stood in his synagogue and unrolled the scroll of the prophet Isaiah, he announced that the call of discipleship is a prophetic awakening: "The Spirit of the Lord is upon me, because he has anointed me to bring good news to the poor. He has sent me to proclaim release to the captives and recovery of sight to the blind, to let the oppressed go free, to proclaim the year of the Lord's favor" (Luke 4:18-19). This is our call, too—to bring good news, to proclaim God's love, and to reach out to those on the margins.

To be a prophet can be an uncomfortable part of the call to discipleship. But it is also what I cannot *not* do as a follower of Christ. What is unjust about our time and place? How are we complicit in systems that contribute to the oppression of others? Where do we need to help call people back to God's ways of mercy, forgiveness, justice, and peace?

All of us need to wake up to the truth. Only then can we walk as prophets in God's light.

Reflection Questions

- If Jesus were to visit your parish, what prophetic message would he give? What do you need to stop doing and what do you need to start doing to embrace the good news of his kingdom?
- Have you ever spoken up for what you believe or taken action in support of a belief or cause that was close to your heart? How did it feel to act prophetically?

- Who are examples of prophetic individuals that inspire you, either from your own life or famous figures? Do you know any young people who are prophetic? Any elders who are unafraid to speak the truth?
- Who is a source of comfort and encouragement to you in your parish community? How have you encouraged others in their prophetic efforts as Christians?
- What are pressing issues in your parish, city, or country that require prophetic witness and action? How might you galvanize attention to these issues?
- Where have you heard God calling you? Where might God be speaking through your life? Where do you feel a stirring or restlessness that might suggest God is leading you somewhere new?

Chapter 8

Steward

Laura Kelly Fanucci

[Jesus said:] "It will be as when a man who was going on a journey called in his servants and entrusted his possessions to them. To one he gave five talents; to another, two; to a third, one—to each according to his ability. Then he went away. Immediately the one who received five talents went and traded with them, and made another five. Likewise, the one who received two made another two. But the man who received one went off and dug a hole in the ground and buried his master's money. After a long time the master of those servants came back and settled accounts with them. The one who had received five talents came forward bringing the additional five. He said, 'Master, you gave me five talents. See, I have made five more.' His master said to him, 'Well done, my good and faithful servant. Since you were faithful in small matters, I will give you great responsibilities. Come, share your master's joy.' [Then] the one who had received two talents also came forward and said, 'Master, you gave me two talents. See, I have made two more.' His master said to him, 'Well done, my good and faithful servant. Since you were faithful in small matters, I will give you great responsibilities. Come, share your master's joy.' Then the one who had received the one talent came forward and said, 'Master, I knew you were a demanding person, harvesting where you did not plant and gathering where you did not scatter; so out of fear I went off and buried your talent in the ground. Here it is back.' His master said to him in reply, 'You wicked, lazy servant! So you knew that I harvest where I did not plant and gather where I did not

> *scatter? Should you not then have put my money in the bank so that I could have got it back with interest on my return? Now then! Take the talent from him and give it to the one with ten. For to everyone who has, more will be given and he will grow rich; but from the one who has not, even what he has will be taken away.'"*
>
> Matthew 25:14-29
> (New American Bible, Revised Edition)

How many times have we heard this gospel proclaimed on Sunday mornings? I remember listening to this passage as a child, mentally calculating it as a math problem: "Five talents plus five talents equals ten; two talents plus two talents equals four. But only one talent buried away equals trouble." Yet if we focus on the final scolding of the fearful servant, we may miss the warm refrain of this parable: "Come, share your master's joy."

At the heart of Jesus' good news about stewardship is a welcoming invitation. Tending to the talents that God has given us is an opportunity for growth. We don't need to hide out of fear or anxiety that we will not be or do enough. What matters is that we care for what we have been given, allowing it to flourish. Stewardship is set forth not as a heavy burden but as a fruitful way of life. We are invited to help tend and nurture our corner of creation. The call to stewardship means receiving gifts gratefully, nurturing their growth, and sharing them with others.

This is how we give back to God.

Jesus the Steward

Stewardship has become an abstract noun today. We often hear the word used to encourage financial support of the church or protection of natural resources. But in Jesus' time, "steward" was a job with clearly defined responsibilities.

The steward was the household manager, overseeing the master's table, property, money, and land. Jesus was described as being God's faithful steward, like Moses before him: "Therefore, brothers and sisters, holy partners in a heavenly calling, consider that Jesus, the apostle and high priest of our confession, was faithful to the one who appointed him, just as Moses also 'was faithful in all God's house'" (Hebrews 3:1-2).

Jesus is the perfect example of stewardship. He cares for God's people. He gives himself as a gift to everyone he encounters. He stewards the vocation to which he has been called, fulfilling his call to serve and to die, emptying himself in obedient love. Jesus links stewardship to discipleship, whether in terms of wealth, power, or authority: "From everyone to whom much has been given, much will be required; and from the one to whom much has been entrusted, even more will be demanded" (Luke 12:48).

Managing Faithfully

Many Catholic parishes have embraced the motto of "time, talent, and treasure" to inspire parishioners to think about stewardship as something more than simply putting money in the collection basket each Sunday. We also contribute to our communities by praying for fellow parishioners, serving in liturgical ministries, working on parish committees, volunteering in social outreach opportunities, and teaching youth in faith formation. But the call to stewardship still goes far beyond the way we serve our parishes. It embraces our professional work, our personal relationships, and our communal concerns.

What or whom do we tend, protect, guide, oversee, or help grow? To be a steward is to manage faithfully, no matter where we find ourselves. Stewardship can be a practice that links the worlds of workplace and home—callings that can pull us in opposite directions in our daily juggle of how to respond to our responsibilities.

Trying to live as a faithful steward also offers a daily reminder that maintenance, not simply creation, is part of vocation. We are called to seek God not only when we do the exciting work of creating something new, but also when we do the ordinary work of caring for what already is. The call to stewardship is the call to take care—of people, of places, and of talents and skills we have been given to share. Like the servants in Jesus' parable, we have been entrusted with God's gifts in the expectation that we will allow them to grow over time. So we are called to be stewards with our whole lives: stewards of our work and of the world around us.

Stewards of Our Work

The first job I took after college was with a French–American company that organized exchange programs for high school students. I had just returned from a year of volunteer work in France, and I thought a natural next step was to continue using my language skills professionally. So when I found a job that offered the perfect opportunity to put my French to work every day, I was thrilled.

Except it did not turn out to be a perfect fit.

I remember driving to the office one morning, creeping through rush hour traffic and wondering, "Is this all there is? Am I just going to keep getting up and going to this job every day for the next however many years of my life?" I turned up the volume on the radio because I didn't want to think about this uneasy question anymore. After all, I had a good-paying job in a tough economy. I had coworkers I liked. I was able to use the talents I had spent four years developing in my undergraduate degree. And I believed in the mission of this organization to foster intercultural understanding. What more could I possibly want?

As the months continued to roll on, I started to see that I had taken this job mostly because of the responsibility I felt toward my education. In doing so, I had set aside other interests in theology and ministry that were now gnawing at me, calling out to be explored. I realized that to be a good steward of all that I had been given—my opportunities, experiences, talents, and interests—I might have to try something else that would bear more fruit in my life. Eventually I went back to graduate school to follow a new path, but not before I spent another year like the fearful servant in Matthew's gospel, paralyzed by anxiety that I was wasting the chance I had been given. Now I can see that I was simply called to care for another part of what God had given me, a new calling that has since borne fruit for myself and those I serve through my work.

Our professional work—or whatever purposeful activity we do to offer our gifts in service to the world—can be part of our response to discipleship's call. Over the past few years, our project has interviewed professionals from diverse fields about their sense of God's calling. Many of them describe how their work has allowed them to be good stewards of their gifts and abilities. Denise, a lawyer and judge, noted that her professional work has given her "so many great opportunities to express what I think are some of the gifts that God gave me for communication and listening and empathy and being the human face of justice to a lot of people." Ken, a woodcarver, offered a series of questions that he uses to discern whether he is stewarding his gifts for the common good: "I have these talents—am I using my talents properly? Or am I overdoing it? Am I more concerned about making money, or more concerned about the power that it gives me or the prestige? Or do I think of it as good for the community and good for my spiritual life?"

What Denise and Ken describe are charisms: gifts we are given to share for the good of the wider community.

As faithful stewards, we are called to nurture our talents, skills, and abilities to respond to the needs of others. Paul's letters to the early Christian communities make this point that gifts from the Spirit must be nurtured for the benefit of the common good: "But each of us was given grace according to the measure of Christ's gift . . . The gifts he gave were that some would be apostles, some prophets, some evangelists, some pastors and teachers, to equip the saints for the work of ministry, for building up the Body of Christ, until all of us come to the unity of the faith and of the knowledge of the Son of God, to maturity, to the measure of the full stature of Christ" (Ephesians 4:7, 11-13). God's gifts are always given for the service of the community that is the household of God: "Like good stewards of the manifold grace of God, serve one another with whatever gift each of you has received" (1 Peter 4:10). When we develop our talents to share with others, we place stewardship at the heart of our work. We contribute to the building up of the Body of Christ.

Stewards of Our World

When we moved into our first home, my husband threw himself into caring for our small property. (I can still hear his mother laughing with disbelief when she saw him digging up a plot of land for a vegetable garden, since he had never expressed any interest in helping tend the family garden while he was growing up!) He was especially excited about the idea of planting fruit trees to make a small orchard. After we had lived in the home for several years, he ordered six apple trees from a local nursery and planted the spindly saplings in two rows in a corner of our yard. By this time, it was clear that we could not be staying in this "starter home" for our whole lives. We hoped to have children one day, and the tiny house was barely big enough for our dog and us. I tried to make this point one night, gently asking if it made sense to put so much time, energy, and financial resources into a home and yard we would not stay in forever. But my husband insisted that "someone else would enjoy these apples." His perspective of stewardship led him to take the long view of caring for the land as an act of faith, not personal gain.

Being a steward comes from being creatures in a created world. God is the first steward of creation, caring for the world and extending this responsibility to humans who are created in God's image. God's command to exercise dominion is an instruction to maintain a proper relationship to creation—to serve, preserve, and cultivate the gifts of the earth. Pope Francis's encyclical *Laudato Si'* sounds a prophetic alarm to address climate change and the impact of industrialization on the natural world. As Jesus describes God's own care for the birds of the air and the grass of the field, so we are called to be careful, compassionate stewards of the land, air, water, and all creatures that live within these environments.

Our stewardship of creation also involves concern for people living in poverty. From the earliest days of Israel's covenant, God's people are called to be a community that cares for the poor, shares personal resources, and praises God as the true source of life and sustenance.

A twentieth-century example of stewardship to people in poverty comes from St. Katharine Drexel. She was the daughter of a wealthy Philadelphia banker who had left his children an inheritance in the millions. Katharine used her portion to care for Native Americans and African Americans, two groups marginalized in American society. Over the years, she gave twelve million dollars from her portion of the estate to missionary activity that established Xavier University in New Orleans—the first Catholic college for Blacks—and one hundred forty-five Catholic missions and twelve schools for Native Americans. Obviously, Katharine was called to steward financial resources far greater than what most of us will face in our lifetime. But her generosity still offers a compelling example of sharing whatever we have been given with those who need it most.

Stewards at Home

My friend Lydia describes caring for her home in terms of stewardship. She and her husband dream of owning their own house, but for now their family finances dictate that renting is more prudent. Yet Lydia takes seriously the call to care for the property around them and finds that when she approaches household maintenance mindfully, she can connect her faith to acts of ordinary work. Lydia once described washing their kitchen walls as a practice of stewardship. Instead of trying to improve the kitchen with a new paint job they could not afford, she spent time caring for what already existed and found that the results could be equally refreshing. Practicing stewardship at home can involve simple acts of caring for our material goods: consuming only what we need, following a budget, and fixing what breaks rather than throwing away what could be repaired.

Following the call to stewardship is a countercultural stance. In our disposable society, convenience rules, and changing trends feed our desires. Even good stewards can be tempted by riches, power, or prosperity—false promises from other gods. In the parable of the rich fool, Jesus warns his followers against selfish hoarding and indulgent exploitation of the gifts God has given: "those who store up treasures for themselves but are not rich toward God" (Luke 12:21). He reminds us that the well-being of our households—as well as the good of our neighbors in need—depends not on accumulating as much as we can for ourselves, but on stewarding our resources and sharing generously, so that all might thrive. Regardless of where we find ourselves, the call to discipleship encourages us to become mindful stewards of our schedules and our salaries as we contribute to the running of our household and workplace.

Paul describes Christians as "servants of Christ and stewards of God's mysteries" (1 Corinthians 4:1). So we are called to be stewards *as part of* our vocation, and stewards *of* our vocations. These are the questions that we must keep asking: What will we manage? Whom will we serve? How will God keep asking us to grow?

Reflection Questions

- Who is someone in your life who embodies the attitude of stewardship? What has their example taught you?
- Consider the refrain of the parable of the faithful servant in Matthew's gospel: "Come, share your master's joy." Where do you experience joy in your life today? How might God be meeting you in these relationships, experiences, or activities to share in your joy?
- Whom do you serve by the talents, skills, and opportunities you have been given?
- Each Sunday at Mass we share monetary gifts at the time of the preparation of the gifts. Imagine that you could place other gifts in the basket—your energy for a particular interest or hobby, your dedication to your work, your commitment to a local charity, or your love for a close friend. What gift could you give back to God that has grown because of your faithful stewardship?

- Stewardship involves seeking what is good in God's eyes. Where in your community do you see God's creation at risk or harmed, such that it needs special stewarding in order to survive and thrive? What can you and your parish or community do to tend to a particular place and restore it?
- Read Pope Francis's encyclical On Care for Our Common Home (*Laudato Si'*), available online from www.vatican.va. How do his reflections on stewardship invite you to take a new perspective on the impact of your life on the natural world around you?

Chapter 9

Conclusion

Laura Kelly Fanucci

[Jesus said:] "Do not let your hearts be troubled. Believe in God, believe also in me. In my Father's house there are many dwelling places. If it were not so, would I have told you that I go to prepare a place for you? And if I go and prepare a place for you, I will come again and will take you to myself, so that where I am, there you may be also. And you know the way to the place where I am going." Thomas said to him, "Lord, we do not know where you are going. How can we know the way?" Jesus said to him, "I am the way, and the truth, and the life. No one comes to the Father except through me."

John 14:1-6

Jesus is the Way. His words to Thomas could not be clearer. When we doubt, he is the truth. When we fear, he is the life. When we wander, he is the Way. He goes ahead of us as he led the first disciples—to prepare good things that await us, to draw us closer to himself, and to lead us into the fullness of God's love. The only reason that we can take up the way of discipleship is because Jesus embodied the fullness of this life before us.

Life on the Way

We are followers, worshipers, witnesses, neighbors, forgivers, prophets, and stewards. But the seven features that we have explored in this book are not seven separate things. They form the one life of discipleship to which God calls us. They are facets of who we are and who God is, as seen in the life of Christ. They are seven ways of *the* way, seven movements of the one path of faith in God.

Think back to a time when you went for a long walk, whether a hike in the mountains, a stroll through a city, a trek through the woods, or a romp in the fields. Remember all the various kinds of walking you did as part of that journey: long strides through open spaces, side steps to descend a slope safely, a restful pace that felt easy to sustain, a quick jog down a steep hill. You might have slowed your pace or sped up to keep in stride with a companion. Your feet might have edged through uncertain terrain or started to drag when you grew tired.

But you were always moving, no matter how you walked.

So too with all the ways we are moving "on the way." Being disciples means that we are in a dynamic relationship with God, who calls, beckons, urges, invites, encourages, and helps us forward. Even as we may shift our focus along the way to respond to different people, places, or circumstances, we are still on the one long walk of discipleship. Drawing connections between the seven features we have explored in this book can help us to see their fundamental unity as part of our calling and identity as Christians.

For example, being worshipers is a natural response to our commitment to being followers of Christ. We cannot help but fall on our knees in wonder, awe, and love for God once we begin to understand what it means to follow Jesus. We also want to share with others what we have learned or how we have grown from following Christ, which leads us to become witnesses. Our witness of what God has done in our lives is shared with those around us as part of our relationship as neighbors. As we learn what it means to be a neighbor to those around us, we come to understand the issues that impact our neighbors' lives, allowing us to speak as prophets on their behalf. Living side by side with our neighbors leads us to become forgivers—another countercultural and prophetic practice. Trying to act and speak prophetically reminds us that we are to be people for others and cannot keep our gifts to ourselves. Sharing our gifts on behalf of our neighbors is our work as stewards, who need the support of a community of other followers as we carry out the call to stewardship in our corner of the world.

Before we become overwhelmed, however, we should remember that we are never called to balance these seven features of discipleship perfectly at any given point in our lives. Instead, the invitation set forth to us as Christians is to center our lives in Christ. This means that certain features of discipleship will emerge as stronger calls, depending on the changing needs and shifting seasons of our lives over time. For example, some people experience the call to be a prophet as a core dimension of their faith as Christians, and they live out this aspect of discipleship every day in their work or community involvement. Other people find that forgiveness in certain relationships ends up taking a significant investment of their energy. During seasons of life when professional work or raising a family are primary concerns, stewardship becomes a lens for understanding our relationship to God and the world. During other seasons, when daily life is not filled with the same pressing responsibilities, we may find more time and space for worship, as seen in the example of older adults who make daily Mass a spiritual practice.

Yet all of us are called to be and called to do as disciples. Our calling is both verb and noun, both identity and action.

Discipleship is not a program to be implemented or a goal to be achieved but a lifelong walk with Christ, who is the Way.

Called as Disciples

Throughout this book we have shared our stories as followers committed to learning the way of Christ. Whether you explored these seven features through discussion with a small group or read the book on your own, we hope that your reflection will join a larger conversation about what it means to be called to discipleship. Whenever we share our stories and connect them with the stories of Scripture, we come to see the power of God at work in our lives. Our stories are part of one larger story: the story of God seeking to draw us closer in love.

This is the heart of vocation—not that we must discover the secret of a single precise purpose that God has determined for our lives, but that we are willing to enter into a lifelong relationship of calling back and forth to God, asking for guidance on how to grow in love and serve those around us.

When we hear the words "vocation" or "calling," we often worry about our personal questions related to work or relationships. But our vocation is not simply about our individual concerns. First and foremost, we are called to share the same way of life as Christians: to be known by our Christlikeness as followers, worshipers, witnesses, neighbors, forgivers, prophets, and stewards. So the natural place to start discerning where and how God calls us is in community.

When we are trying to sort through questions related to our callings, we may turn to a trusted friend, pastor, or spiritual advisor to help guide us. We might join a small group to explore with others where we experience God's presence. We may study a new form of prayer (like *lectio divina*) to attune our heart to God's word. But no matter how we bring our vocational concerns into conversation with the community and traditions of the church, we can be confident that we are in the company of others seeking to know and do God's will. This is the gift of being called together on the way of discipleship. We journey together with the risen Christ, who is the Way, the Truth, and the Life.

Called for Mission

In our common call as disciples we share a common mission. Jesus' great commission to his followers at the end of Matthew's gospel is the same invitation set before us today: "Go therefore and make disciples of all nations" (Matthew 28:19). We do this work of spreading the mission of Christ by living out these seven features of discipleship so that we can share God's love with those we meet. Like the first disciples, we are sent forth into the world to be followers, worshipers, witnesses, neighbors, forgivers, prophets, and stewards.

Every time we practice one of these features of discipleship —by our words, our actions, or simply our presence—we also "re-member" ourselves back into the Body of Christ, which is the church. As members of a local community of the church, we can encourage each other in each of these features of discipleship by our friendship, our support, and our prayers whenever we gather to worship God in the Eucharist. Jesus' final comforting words that follow his challenging commission remind us that we will never be left alone as we work toward the church's mission here on earth: "And remember, I am with you always, to the end of the age" (Matthew 28:20). As you continue to reflect on the call to discipleship, may you find courage and strength in Christ's faithful promise to those who follow him on the way.

Appendix 1

A Guide to Lectio Divina

Lectio divina, or "holy reading," is an ancient practice from the Christian tradition, dating from the early medieval era of prayerful study of Scripture in monasteries. This prayer practice has been used by Christians since St. Benedict described *lectio divina* in his Rule around the year 500.

Lectio divina is a slow, quiet, and thoughtful encounter with Scripture. It aims to help us discern what God is calling us to be and to do, as we listen for God's voice through the stories of Scripture.

Based on the image of Jacob's ladder, a twelfth-century Carthusian monk named Guigo II described four steps of *lectio divina*: *lectio* (reading), *meditatio* (meditation), *oratio* (prayer), and *contemplatio* (contemplation). Through these four steps, God's word sinks deeper into our hearts and imagination.

But *lectio divina* is different from Bible study. We let the Scripture passage stand alone, without additional explanation or commentary, because *lectio divina* is an encounter between God's word and our lives. Slowly reading and reflecting on the biblical passage three times provides time and space for God's word to move from our lips, into our minds, and finally into our hearts.

Find a quiet place for your reflection. Begin in prayer: "Lord, open my heart to reflect on your call in my life and for my life. Amen."

Read the Scripture passage aloud for the first time. Spend a few moments in silence reflecting on the passage. What word or phrase strikes you? Hold that word or phrase in your mind as you spend a few moments in quiet reflection.

Read the Scripture passage aloud for the second time, holding in mind the word or phrase that struck you when you first read it. What might God be saying to you through this word or phrase? Spend a few moments in quiet reflection.

Read the Scripture passage aloud for a third and final time. How might God be calling you to act through the word or phrase that first struck you? How might you respond to this call?

Sit with the Scripture passage for another minute in quiet reflection and thanksgiving. Then close with a final prayer: "Lord, open my heart to reflect on your call in my life and for my life. Amen."

We invite you to try this prayer practice as a way of deepening your dialogue with God as you go through *Called on the Way*. Over time, *lectio divina* can become a prayer that opens your heart to hear how God is speaking in your everyday life. As you become comfortable with this form of prayer, you might try taking the word or phrase that spoke to you from the week's Scripture and holding it in mind as you go about your day, praying with the word or phrase at the start and end of each day.

Kathleen uses this approach in "Daily Lectio" on the Ritual - Wellbeing Practices app, which follows the daily Lectionary.

Appendix 2

How to Use Called on the Way *in a Small Group*

Called on the Way can be used in parishes as a book club selection or a study guide for small-group reflection. Each of the seven chapters can be read and discussed as part of a seven-week program on discipleship.

Advent and Lent offer opportunities to launch a small group, as well as the seven weeks between Easter and Pentecost. A facilitator should ideally aim to gather a minimum of six to eight participants to encourage good discussion and keep group meetings under two hours.

Called on the Way can also be read by youth preparing for confirmation, candidates in the Order of Christian Initiation of Adults (or OCIA, formerly known as RCIA), young adults, parents' groups, retirees, or others in the parish interested in exploring questions of calling and faith.

Praying

Begin your group's time together with a group prayer of *lectio divina* using the Scripture passage at the beginning of the week's chapter. (See appendix 1 for an outline of *lectio divina*. Guidelines for group *lectio divina* and a printable handout can also be found in the *Called to Life* Facilitator Guide at www.called-to-life.com.) You may also wish to sing an opening hymn related to the meeting's theme.

Reflecting

Start with a brief summary of the chapter's main points to review what participants read in preparation for your time together. You may wish to show a *Lives Explored* video in order to open conversation. (Appendix 3 offers a list of related videos.) The majority of the group's time can be spent discussing the reflection questions at the end of the chapter. You may not have time to cover all questions, but these should offer enough prompts to get participants thinking and sharing about how they live out this aspect of discipleship in their daily work and relationships with God and others.

Sending Forth

At the end of your meeting, encourage participants to consider where they might be called to live out this aspect of discipleship in the next week. Offer each person the opportunity to name how they plan to focus on the feature of discipleship, whether through a concrete action, a change in attitude, or a commitment to prayer. End with a prayer of gratitude for the time and stories shared. You may wish to close by having the group sing another hymn on discipleship or by another reading of the opening Scripture passage.

Blessing

The following prayer can be offered as a final blessing to participants at the end of each meeting:

May God bless you with ears to listen
to the still small voice.
May you have strength to follow Christ's call
to be his disciple.
May you discern the Spirit's bountiful gifts
showered upon you.
And may you live a life of service for others,
in joy and gratitude.

Appendix 3

Resources on Vocation and Calling

Called on the Way draws from the work of the Collegeville Institute Seminars, an ecumenical research project that brings together theologians, ministers, and social scientists to explore important issues facing today's Christian communities, a project of the Collegeville Institute located at Saint John's University in Collegeville, Minnesota. Through this work, and in collaboration with other organizations and churches working on calling over the past fifteen years, resources for congregations, seminaries, universities, and other places of ministry can be found here: https://calledtolives.com/vocation/ and https://www.communitiesofcalling.org/congregational-resources/.

Laura created two programs on calling including facilitators' guides, which may be helpful for those guiding small groups using *Called on the Way*. We invite you to explore the facilitator resources available at www.called-to-life.com and www.called-to-work.com.

We also created video interviews with people sharing stories of their experience of God's call in their lives, work, and relationships. The *Lives Explored* videos are available from the Seminars' website (www.lives-explored.com) and the *Lives Explored* YouTube channel. Below is a list of *Lives Explored* videos that connect with each feature of discipleship explored in *Called on the Way*. You may wish to show a video (either as a clip or in its entirety) as a conversation starter for a small group meeting. Videos can also be viewed for personal reflection to offer additional perspectives on the seven features of discipleship.

- **Follower**: Angela speaks about looking for God's road signs as she follows her calling to creativity from professional work to parenting.
- **Worshiper**: Sherice speaks about praising God with prayer and song both in church and in her workplace.
- **Witness**: Mary Margaret and Ken share their story of keeping faith throughout their journey with Alzheimer's in order to help others who face this difficult diagnosis.
- **Neighbor**: Jane remembers God's promise to send her the people she needs as she considers a new calling to serve neighbors outside her comfort zone.
- **Forgiver**: Joyce describes her journey to self-forgiveness in moving beyond negative voices from her past and embracing the confidence of a new calling.
- **Prophet**: Adam speaks about his passion for helping teens create powerful plays about provocative social issues.
- **Steward**: Ken asks questions about stewardship related to his calling as a woodworker, seeking to offer his gifts in service to others.

Appendix 4

Resources for Further Reading

Brueggemann, Walter, and Patrick Miller. *The Word That Redescribes the World: The Bible and Discipleship*. Minneapolis: Fortress Press, 2011.

Cahalan, Kathleen A. *Introducing the Practice of Ministry*. Collegeville, MN: Liturgical Press, 2010.

Cahalan, Kathleen A. *Stories We Live: Finding God's Calling All around Us*. Grand Rapids, MI: Wm. B. Eerdmans, 2017.

Coombs, Marie Theresa, and Francis Kelly Nemeck. *Called by God: A Theology of Vocation and Lifelong Commitment*. Collegeville, MN: Liturgical Press, 1992.

Fanucci, Laura Kelly. *Everyday Sacrament: The Messy Grace of Parenting*. Collegeville, MN: Liturgical Press, 2014.

Fanucci, Laura Kelly. *To Bless Our Callings: Prayers, Poems, and Hymns to Celebrate Vocation*. Eugene, OR: Wipf & Stock, 2017.

Fortin, Jack. *The Centered Life: Awakened, Called, Set Free, and Nurtured*. Minneapolis: Augsburg Fortress, 2006.

Hahnenberg, Edward. *Awakening Vocation: A Theology of Christian Call*. Collegeville, MN: Liturgical Press, 2010.

Langford, Jeremy, and James Martin. *Professions of Faith: Living and Working as a Catholic*. Franklin, WI: Sheed & Ward, 2002.

Neafsey, John. *A Sacred Voice Is Calling: Personal Vocation and Social Conscience*. Maryknoll, NY: Orbis Books, 2006.

Palmer, Parker. *Let Your Life Speak: Listening for the Voice of Vocation*. San Francisco: Jossey-Bass, 2000.

Placher, William C., ed. *Callings: Twenty Centuries of Christian Wisdom on Vocation*. Grand Rapids, MI: Wm. B. Eerdmans, 2005.

Reyes, Patrick. *Nobody Cries When We Die: God, Community, and Surviving to Adulthood.* St. Louis, MO: Chalice Press, 2018.

Schuurman, Douglas. *Vocation: Discerning Our Callings in Life*. Grand Rapids, MI: Wm. B. Eerdmans, 2004.

Schwehn, Mark R., and Dorothy C. Bass, eds. *Leading Lives That Matter: What We Should Do and Who We Should Be*. 2nd. ed. Grand Rapids, MI: Wm. B. Eerdmans, 2020.

Authors' Information

Kathleen A. Cahalan is professor of practical theology at Saint John's Graduate School of Theology and Seminary, where she teaches courses on pastoral ministry, pastoral care, and spirituality. As senior research fellow at Collegeville Institute, she directed a ten-year collaborative research project that studied various aspects of vocation. She coedited two volumes from the project: *Calling All Years Good: Vocation throughout Life's Seasons* (Wm. B. Eerdmans, 2017) and *Calling in Today's World: Voices from Eight Faith Perspectives* (Wm. B. Eerdmans, 2016). She has also authored books for church audiences, including *Stories We Live: Finding God's Calling All around Us* (Wm. B. Eerdmans, 2017) and *Living Your Discipleship: Seven Ways to Express Your Deepest Calling*, coauthored with Laura Kelly Fanucci (Twenty-Third Publications, 2015). She has served as the coordinator for the Lilly Endowment's Called to Lives of Meaning and Purpose Initiative from 2018 to 2022. She practices *lectio divina* with the Lectionary readings on the app Ritual - Wellbeing Practices.

Laura Kelly Fanucci is an author, speaker, and founder of *Mothering Spirit*, where she first started writing about parenting and spirituality in 2010. She earned her BA from the University of Notre Dame and her master of divinity from Saint John's School of Theology. Laura has authored seven books, including *Everyday Sacrament: The Messy Grace of Parenting* (Liturgical Press, 2014) and *Grieving Together: A Couple's Journey through Miscarriage* (Our Sunday Visitor, 2018). She is also author of three volumes in the Little Rock

Scripture Study series Alive in the Word: *Grief, Finding Hope in Sorrow*; *Mercy, God's Nature, Our Challenge*; and *Dashed Hopes, When Our Best-Laid Plans Fall Apart.* Laura's work has been featured on the Hallow and Ritual - Wellbeing Practices apps, and in popular outlets including NPR's *Morning Edition, On Being*, and the *Kelly Clarkson Show*. She writes frequently for online and print publications including OSV News Service, Grotto Network, and *Give Us This Day*. She and her husband live in Minnesota with their children.